The Joy
of
Working

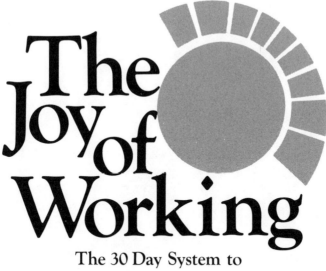

The Joy of Working

The 30 Day System to
Success, Wealth, & Happiness
on the Job

Denis Waitley, Ph. D.
& Reni L. Witt

A Larimi Communications Book
DODD, MEAD & COMPANY
New York

Copyright © 1985 by Larimi Communications Associates, Inc.

All rights reserved

No part of this book may be reproduced in any form
without permission in writing from the publisher.
Published by Dodd, Mead & Company, Inc.
79 Madison Avenue, New York, N.Y. 10016
Distributed in Canada by
McClelland and Stewart Limited, Toronto
Manufactured in the United States of America

Designed by Claire Counihan

First Edition

Library of Congress Cataloging in Publication Data

Waitley, Denis.
   The joy of working.

   (A Larimi Communications book)
   1. Job satisfaction.   I. Witt, Reni L., 1953–
II. Title.   III. Series.
HF5549.5.J63W17   1985   650.1'4   84-25931
ISBN 0-396-08508-3

CONTENTS

[v]

CONTENTS

To my wife, Susan, who makes work a celebration.

D.W.

To my husband, Jeffrey Kriz, for the joy he brings me.

R.W.

SPECIAL THANKS

Our most grateful appreciation to Michael M. Smith for his vision and inspiration, Celeste Hall for her spirit and support, and Cynthia Vartan for her astute editorial guidance. Their joy of working made this book a joy to write.

PROLOGUE

Most of our adult lives are spent working. Taking into account commuting time, overtime, thinking about our jobs, and worrying over work, we spend more of our waking hours in the office, at the factory, on the road, behind the desk than we do at home.

But too many of us find our jobs dull, laborious, and repetitive, an irritating necessity of life, like death and taxes. How many people have said, "I like the work but hate my job," or "How can I like my work? It's just a job," or "The only joy I get at work is when the little hand on the clock says it's five o'clock."

This is a reality shared by countless workers, but the above remarks were made by a high-ranking corporate executive. His salary is in the six figures, he keeps three secretaries busy, and oversees the work of five hundred employees from behind his great mahogany desk. You may envy his job. You might think, "Nice work, if you can get it." Yet this executive finds his work taxing, stressful, repetitive, and tedious. Whatever initial enthusiasm he had to achieve his early goals, along the way he lost it.

It's true for so many of us. Whether blue collar, pink collar, or white collar, workers across the country feel frustrated and unsatisfied on the job.

"The *joy* of working?" we heard many of our friends say. "That's got to be a joke."

Jim Mitchell, a television journalist in Louisville, Kentucky, hit the nail on the head: "Too many workers would rather get home than get ahead."

The media have picked up on America's lack of enthusiasm for working, citing problems of poor quality, reduced productivity, and declining services. In an attempt to find some answers, management experts have turned outside of our own country and culture. They come back with the exemplar of the Japanese worker, happy, healthy, better motivated, devoted to the company job. But the rigid conformity and dronelike discipline is ultimately counterproductive to innovation and progress. Put more succinctly, it's just not the American way of doing things.

So, as we began writing this book, we had to ask ourselves this question: Is it possible to combine *excellence*—quality, productivity, service—with *enjoyment?* We reviewed dozens of studies, reports, and books, but nearly all of them were geared to the corporate climber and the business manager. What about the vast majority of wage-earning Americans? Can everyone from the mailboy to the secretary to the junior executive to the C.E.O. *excel by enjoying work?*

We firmly believe the answer is:

YES! Every American has the right and the ability to find joy of working. What we have forgotten is that *the key to personal progress, profit, and productivity is enjoyment!*

That realization was the turning point that started us to work on this book. Although we come from totally different backgrounds and have had different life and career experiences, we found that we shared the same basic ideas about joy and about work. Our conversations together over several years synergized into a philosophy that evolved into the building blocks of the joy of working.

- Don't anticipate the worst—expect the best.
- A problem is a problem only if *you* want it to be. You can transform a problem into an opportunity.
- Focus on where you want to go rather than where you're coming from.
- Learn from your *successes* as well as from your mistakes.
- Real success has little to do with a gifted birth, outstanding talent, or high intelligence.
- It makes little difference what's happening out there. *It's how you take it and what you make of it that counts.*
- Happiness is not something owed you. Nobody is handed joy on a silver platter. Instead, you make your own happiness, knowing it is an attitude, a habit gained from daily practice.

The joy of working is more than a philosophy; it's a system to finding enjoyment, wealth, and success on the job. Each chapter contains one essential key, one central "thought for the day" to open the door of personal prosperity.

We built the system on a fundamental cornerstone: self-esteem. There can be no progress in the workplace until an individual values himself and feels valued by others. That's the foundation of all human fulfillment. From this beginning, we move step by step, day by day, to each of the major keys essential to enjoyment and excellence on the job. Starting with the basics, such as *Goal Setting, Self-expectation, Being Your Best,* we progress to the next stage, including *Opportunity, Motivation, Priorities,* then on to the pinnacles of our work system, *Faith, Wealth, Wisdom,* and *Success*. Finally we come to the ultimate purpose of our life and work: *Joy*.

Each chapter is connected to the one preceding it and leads up to the following one. Yet each chapter stands independently, to be turned to as a reference and guide.

We devised the book to be read one day at a time. One short chapter each morning to energize and build upon. This is a book to read, reread, underline, highlight, be inspired by, and share with co-workers, employees, the boss, friends, and family members.

The Joy of Working is not a fad book or a one-shot, quick-fix solution to problems of low productivity, poor morale, and job-related unhappiness. This is not a book for intimidators, manipulators, or the hard-core driven who claw for "success." The joy of working does not mean turning into a "workaholic" as some books have advocated. Nor does it mean becoming a doormat to your boss, your co-workers, or the "bottom line."

Instead, *The Joy of Working* is a *do-it-yourself daily life guide*—a practical system full of truths and values that can carry you through not only the eight-hour day, but also through your time at home with friends and loved ones. It's a book to be used every day of the week, every week of the month, every month of your working career.

Whether you are a business manager, secretary, computer programmer, sales representative, engineer, office manager, factory worker, actor, athlete, teacher, or homemaker, we hope that you'll find on each page insights and attitudes that can lead you to find joy in the work you do. This thirty-day system will unlock your potential to turn your personal ideals of success and happiness into reality.

It is our heartfelt wish that in discovering the joy of working, you'll become a happier and more self-actualized person. You'll feel in control of your work and your environment. You'll stretch, realizing you have more capabilities and talents than you ever imagined. In short, the joy of working system means experiencing joy not just on weekends and holidays but *every* day.

As we've suggested, you don't need a lot of motivation or an M.B.A. from Harvard to benefit from this book. The joy of working system is not dependent on an inherited bank account, intelligence quotient, the right schools, big promotions, expense accounts, physical beauty, race, color, or social status. What sets *The Joy of Working* apart from all other so-called "motivational" books is the "joy" factor, which can make any job more productive, more satisfying, more enjoyable.

Mark Twain once wrote, "The higher the pay in enjoyment the worker gets out of [his labors], the higher shall be his pay in money also." He called it "The Law of Work." We call it The Joy of Working.

By following the day-by-day system in this book, you'll discover how you can achieve success, wealth, and happiness—starting today!

All you have to do is turn the page—

DAY

1

Self-esteem

YOU ARE a Most Valuable Person in your work.
Repeat it.
You are a Most Valuable Person in your work.
It's true.

You are a most valuable person. No one else can quite fill your shoes. No one else can be you. You bring your unique being to work every day. You bring with you your talents, your abilities, your knowledge, your skills, your personality, or just your plain know-how. You may not be using all of your abilities just yet. You may not be using them to the fullest. You may not even recognize how valuable a person you are.

Are you saying to yourself right now, "Oh, I'm not important. Many people do what I do," or "What I do is not so valuable," or "Well, I'm the account manager, but I had connections. Anyone can do what I do."

The type of work you do, your title, or your salary has actually very little to do with the cornerstone of the joy of working system: *self-esteem.*

WHAT IS SELF-ESTEEM?

Self-esteem is the first key to finding happiness on the job. Self-esteem is the cornerstone of success. It's that deep-down feeling in your soul of your own self-worth. Individuals who enjoy their work develop strong beliefs of self-worth and self-confidence. They weren't necessarily born with these good feelings. They might have even been made to feel clumsy and stupid in their youth. But as working adults, they *learned* to like themselves through practice.

------◆◆●◆—◆------

Often-times nothing profits more than self-esteem, grounded on what is just and right.

JOHN MILTON

------◆◆●◆—◆------

Healthy self-esteem is not narcissistic, self-indulgent, or arrogant. Healthy self-esteem means to appreciate the value of yourself as a unique human being with your own special talents and abilities. Indeed, the word "esteem" is founded in Latin, meaning "to value highly."

It would be impossible to value another person without first feeling value for yourself. When you place value on your own work and efforts, you can begin to find the value in the work of others. It's in your power to encourage self-esteem and well-being at your place of work. You can feel self-esteem even though you may not have done anything yet, but simply because you have the capability for it.

[3]

A JOB WELL-DONE

Many successful men and women derive their self-esteem from their work. They know that a job well-done leaves an inner glow of satisfaction. It's not always necessary that the world knows of your achievement. Nor does it really matter whether the result was a failure or a success. What is important is that *you* know you have tried your best. You gave the task at hand your all.

Some workers, however, hold the philosophy: "Get away with the most while doing the least possible." Contrary to popular mores, this negative attitude actually requires more thought and energy than doing your best. Further, practicing this negative approach to your work *depletes* your sense of self-esteem, for deep inside, you know you have not lived up to the best that is within you.

THE SELF-IMAGE HIGHWAY TO SUCCESS

Have you ever said to yourself—

- I can't imagine myself being successful.
- I would like to, but I don't have enough experience/the right education.
- I can't get ahead because I'm too short, overweight, a woman, a black, my parents were poor.

The truth is, most people talk themselves into failure and dejection. The result is the Fear of Trying.

Most of us know of or have read about common, everyday people who have become uncommonly productive and successful in their work and careers; individuals who have overcome enormous outer obstacles and inner roadblocks to become great.

Yet many people can't imagine doing such things themselves. They say, "Yes, he could do it or she's doing it, but I can't because ———."

They develop the habit of failure. It takes two forms:

Failure Reinforcement—the habit of looking back at past problems.

Failure Forecasting—the habit of imagining the worst in the future.

Because they lack sufficient self-esteem to believe in the validity of their dreams, they don't prepare for their achievement, and therefore are going down a dead-end street. No wonder so many people who work feel trapped. Failure becomes set in their self-images.

———————◆—◗◦◖—◆———————

Never put yourself down—the workplace is full of put-downs. Don't do it to yourself.

———————◆—◗◦◖—◆———————

SELF-ESTEEM TAKES PRACTICE

Believe in yourself, no matter how long it takes or how tough it may seem at times. There was once a college professor whose wife had a hearing deficiency. In trying to invent a device to enhance her hearing, he created something more complex that he thought might be useful to the public. He traveled throughout the New England states trying to find venture capital to take his idea into production. But businessmen everywhere laughed at him. "Ideas are a dime a dozen," they said. "The project's doomed to failure." They told him that the human voice could never travel through a wire. Thank goodness Alexander Graham Bell had the self-esteem to hang in there even when his only reward was his belief in himself.

Often, we put imaginary barriers in our path when no such barrier exists. In the 1940s, the greatest physicists and aeronautical engineers believed that the sound barrier could not be broken, that anyone or anything would be shattered when it approached the speed of sound. One lone pilot, Chuck Yeager, didn't believe it. He didn't think there was such a thing as a sound "barrier." And indeed, he flew right through it.

THE JOY OF WORKING IN ACTION

1. Always greet your co-workers, your boss, your subordinates with a smile. As simple as it sounds, a smile establishes your own self-worth and shares it with others. Successful people almost always smile at the people they come across at work.

2. When answering the phone or placing calls at work, be pleasant. Smile with your voice. Always give your name immediately, and if the other person doesn't know you, give your company's name and briefly state the reason for your call. This simple practice underscores that a *person of value* is calling.

3. Always say "Thank You" when you are praised at work. No need to belittle or play down your

achievement; no need to either elaborate or fish for further praise. A simple "thank you" is the universal mark of an individual with self-esteem.

4. You don't have to wear the labels others try to give you. If you feel needlessly belittled, ridiculed, or rejected by someone at work, recognize this not as a failure on your part, but as ignorance and lack of self-esteem on the part of the other person.

5. Stay away from "pity parties" or "gripe sessions." It may feel like worker "solidarity" but it's actually climbing aboard a sinking ship. Instead, find successful and happy role models to pattern yourself after. Surround yourself with people who enjoy their work. People with self-esteem seem to radiate it to others.

You'll gain self-esteem and joy on the job by beginning each morning with the thought that:

You Are
A
Most Valuable Person.

DAY

2

Self-talk

IN Day One, we examined the importance of self-esteem as the foundation for enjoying your job. When you mentally repeat to yourself a phrase such as "I am a most valuable person," you are already putting into practice the second principle of the Joy of Working system: *self-talk*.

The practice of positive self-talk is perhaps the most important key to the permanent enhancement of self-esteem. To feel good about ourselves and our work, we must constantly feed our self-image with positive thoughts about our accomplishments and performance.

To enjoy our jobs we need to use constructive feedback in the form of self-talk every day.

YOUR INNER VIDEO CASSETTE

Whether we realize it or not, each of us carries in our mind an "inner video cassette." It's a very complicated video cassette containing (by the time we're thirty years old) some three trillion pictures of ourselves. This inner cassette may not be consciously recognizable, but it exists in each of us.

This self-image recorder has been built by our own beliefs and thoughts about ourselves. It records images of what we see and what other people say. More importantly, it records our self-talk, minute to minute.

We all talk to ourselves in words, pictures, and emotions at three to four hundred words a minute. Every waking moment we mold our self-esteem with thoughts about ourselves and our performances at work.

Become aware of the silent conversations you hold with yourself. Even if you don't consciously realize it, you are constantly judging and prejudging your every action. Your self-talk is creating your self-image.

YOUR SELF-TALK *IS* YOUR SELF-IMAGE

Some years ago an article in *Reader's Digest* told of an experiment conducted with a class of high school basketball players. These young men with similar skills were divided into three separate groups. Group One was told not to practice shooting free throws in the gym for a month. Group Two was told to practice shooting free throws in the gym for an hour every afternoon for a month. Group Three was told to practice shooting free throws *in their imaginations* for an hour every afternoon for a month.

At the end of the month, the players were tested for their performance. As expected, Group One's free-throw average fell. Group Two increased its average by about two percentage points. Surprisingly, Group Three also *increased* its average by the same percentage as Group Two.

DAY 2

In your imagination, you never miss—that is, unless you want to or unless you're in the habit of negative self-imaging.

Negative self-talk can follow a success or a failure. For example, when you close a sale or turn in a report on time, your negative self-talk afterward might be "Gee, that was a lucky one," or "I sure hope I don't miss the deadline next time."

On the other hand, if you lose a sale or make a mistake or deliver an assignment late, negative self-talk might be "What a klutz I am," or "There I go again. I'll never get it right." Self-talk disintegrates into "I knew I couldn't do it," "This always happens to me," "Why do I even try?" Just as important as your self-imaging before a task, your self-talk immediately after confirms your self-image or knocks it down.

But, after a mistake or failure, the person who has learned the principle of positive self-talk will say, "That's not like me," "Next time I'll take a different approach," "I'll get up and do it again, but this time I'll prepare more effectively."

In a way, learning how to succeed in spite of failure is like learning how to walk. The effort results in a number of falls, bumps, near misses, and landing on your rear end (figuratively speaking, of course, in the adult worker). The difference is that the child does not associate falling with failure, but only as a temporary inconvenience. The child's next thought is to get up and try it again.

So it should be with us. We set a goal in our minds, we try, we fall, we see the goal again, perhaps with renewed vigor or from a different angle, our self-talk reinforces the desire to succeed, and ultimately we do. This experience is then stored in our inner video cassettes to replay when we next need to.

REPLAY WHAT'S RIGHT WITH YOU

Unhappy people who hate their jobs, their work, their lives, constantly flip on their inner videos to programs that show failure. They watch old reruns of past hurts, missed opportunities, and botched assignments.

People who enjoy working play back over and over again the times they did things right. They vividly remember small successes, the appreciative compliment, a job well-done. Particularly when faced with stress, frustration, or failure, they press an "instant replay" in their minds, bringing up these positive mental images. Such positive inner reinforcement provides optimism and opportunity to overcome the problem. Afterward, the experience is stored as another example of "what's right with you."

Positive self-talk after a performance is just as important to building self-esteem as positive self-talk beforehand. Replaying what's right with you in words, pictures, and emotions adds to the joy of working.

SELF-TALK IN ACTION

1. Use *positive* adjectives and adverbs when you talk to others about yourself. More importantly, use positive language when you talk to yourself. Your thoughts and your words should work together to uplift your spirit.

2. Write a one-page résumé of your professional and personal assets. List all your skills, your experiences, and your potential. In other words, write down what you're good at. Refer to this one-page autobiography once a week. It's the script for your self-talk.

DAY 2

3. Set aside a few minutes each day to visualize yourself achieving and enjoying your most personal desires. Picture yourself closing a sale, getting a promotion, receiving a raise. Experience in your mind how good the professional triumph feels. You've just added another tape for instant replay on your inner video.

4. Part of being human is having bad days and making mistakes. When you feel you've not done your best, your self-talk should be "That's not like me. I can do better than that. Next time I'll try harder/try a different way." Then replay the action correctly in your imagination.

Positive self-talk is a learned habit. It takes daily practice. The second key to the joy of working is taking time each day to:

Replay & Reinforce What's Right With You.

DAY

Attitude

HEALTHY self-esteem and positive self-talk are the spiritual seeds of happiness and success. Now is the time to get those seeds to sprout. The necessary nutrient for joy is *attitude.*

Positive attitudes are like nourishment to the body and soul. The right attitude can carry you through the worst days at work.

On the other hand, negative attitudes are absolutely poisonous to the body. Any chance for happiness can be suffocated by negativism. Negative thinking patterns can actually lead to physical illness and emotional destitution.

Does that sound exaggerated? It's not. And science now has the link.

THE OPIATES OF OPTIMISM

Recent discoveries in psychopharmacology relate directly to the theory of why a positive mental attitude is one of the single most important traits toward achieving health and happiness.

Medical researchers have discovered that the body produces natural morphinelike substances that operate on specific receptor sites in the brain and spinal cord. These natural, internal opiates are called endorphins. Secreted and used by the brain, endorphins reduce the experience of pain and screen out unpleasant stimuli. In fact, the presence of endorphins actually causes the feeling of well-being.

Studies on clinically depressed patients show a severe lack of the endorphin chemical. This may be the beginning of a breakthrough in understanding the origins of depression and joy. It might very well be that happy, optimistic people have an abundance of this natural opiate flowing through their bodies.

More importantly, behavioral researchers are learning that *we can actually stimulate the production of endorphins through optimistic thoughts and a positive attitude.*

THE VICTOR'S CIRCLE

You've heard of the "vicious circle" in which one problem gives rise to another problem, leading back to the first problem. Negative thinking deprives the body of endorphins, leading to depression, leading back to more negative thinking.

Now, let's reverse the process. There is growing scientific evidence that positive mental attitudes actually create a natural "high" to help the individual withstand pain, overcome depression, turn stress into energy, and gather the strength to persevere.

In one related study, actors were wired to electrodes and hooked to blood catheters. They were then asked to perform various scenes. When they portrayed characters who were angry or depressed or without hope, endorphin levels dropped. But when the scene called for emoting joy, confidence, and love, endorphins shot up.

Science has shown that positive thoughts produce endorphins. Endorphins in turn encourage feelings of optimism and well-being.

[19]

These feelings reinforce positive attitudes. This is what we call the "Victor's Circle."

ATTITUDE IS INFECTIOUS

Each one of us is responsible for his or her own actions and attitudes. People who are happy, satisfied with themselves, successful in getting what they want from life are self-made. Their positive attitudes make them what they are.

A positive attitude is as important for the secretary behind her office desk as it is for the salesman on the showroom floor. Enthusiasm is contagious. It's difficult to remain neutral or indifferent in the presence of a positive thinker. He or she radiates energy, good humor, and motivation. The person with the ability to look on the brighter side of life establishes a camaraderie, an *esprit de corps* among fellow workers. It's easy to become infected by this wonderful, positive outlook.

Your attitude is a choice you make.

THE WRONG STUFF

Has anyone ever said to you, "You've got the wrong attitude," or "I don't like your attitude"?

When it happens, your natural reaction may be to act defensively, sometimes even hostilely, which only fuels the fire to the accusation, "You've got the wrong attitude."

Negative attitudes spread like flames in a forest fire. They can literally destroy a company—scorch interpersonal relationships, singe the growth of creativity, char the efforts of an entire project. One person with a pervasively negative attitude can do this. Whether that worker is a manager or a mailboy, the effect on others is the same.

But the person who is burned most severely is not the object of the negativism—the boss or co-worker or subordinate. The person most damaged by negativism is the individual who harbors that wrong stuff within him.

He is probably a profoundly unhappy individual, racked by frustration and loneliness. It's a painful truth that people instinctively stay away from negative, pessimistic, grudging losers.

Negative thinking patterns also affect the health of the individual. Without a steady flow of endorphins produced by positive attitudes, the body has no defense against everyday stress, disappointments, and losses. Doctors now know that these emotions can be linked to almost every disease from the common cold to cancer.

People without a positive attitude are often drawn to external means to cure their depression: alcohol, marijuana, tranquilizers, cocaine, food binges, shopping sprees, promiscuity, and gambling.

Is the individual smoldering with negativism doomed to be consumed in his own despair? The answer is a resounding NO. There is hope.

We've talked about self-imaging. Self-imaging is a twentieth-century concept founded on Biblical wisdom. In the Book of Proverbs is written, "As he thinketh in his heart, so is he."

As you think, so you are.

Since you have the ability to control your thoughts, you can change.

YOU ARE IN CHARGE

You are in charge of your life. You are in control of your attitude. It's not your boss, your job, your parents, the breaks that create your attitude. It's you. How you think and how you react is totally up to you.

Looking for bad things to happen can actually make them happen. People with negative attitudes generally expect such situations as losing a job, bankruptcy, poor employee relations, unpleasant working conditions, and failure. Pessimists expect to feel bad and get sick, so they do.

On the other hand, reality-oriented positive thinking can influence us to overcome significant obstacles.

If you really believe a goal can be reached, your attitude releases new energy that actually can help bring about the achievement of the goal.

During every moment of your life, you program your attitude to work for you or against you. Attitude itself is a neutral mechanism. It's only a means to an end. Whatever your objectives and goals are, their direction is set by your attitudes, whether they are positive or negative, true or false, right or wrong, self-enhancing or self-destroying. Your attitude creates the outcome according to *your* instructions, much like a computer printing out according to its inputs.

Positive images can bolster you even when everything is going wrong. And until you've found a solution to the problem, or the situation changes, you've maintained your energy. You've not caved in. You've *survived.*

In the face of an obstacle, your inner attitude will shine through to your outer behavior, catapulting you over to ultimate success.

---◆—◆•◆—◆---

We are not responsible for what happens out there, what others do or think. We are responsible only for how we choose to respond. That's our attitude. The responsibility for us is ours.

---◆—◆•◆—◆---

IS YOUR JOB A SCAPEGOAT?

In the Old Testament, the Book of Leviticus tells of a sacred custom called the "escaped goat." When the troubles of the people became too much, a healthy male goat was brought into the temple. In a solemn ceremony, the highest priest of the tribe placed his hands on the head of the goat and recited the list of woes. The problems were then transferred onto the goat and the goat was set free, taking the troubles away with him.

That was about 4,000 years ago, but we still use " 'scape" goats today. We frequently use other people, other things in our lives to avoid accepting the responsibility of who we are and what we do. Instead of working on what is going on inside us, we try to blame that which is around us.

It's always easier and more convenient to assume the answer lies elsewhere or with others. When life gets tough at work, we start to think, "It's this job." We often use our job as a scapegoat for the "wrong stuff" circulating inside us.

BUILD A CATHEDRAL

Attitude at work can be summarized by this wonderful story, told by Edward Pulling, a great educator.

Back in the Middle Ages, a dispatcher went out to determine

how laborers felt about their work. He went to a building site in France.

He approached the first worker and asked, "What are you doing?"

"What are you, blind?" the worker snapped back. "I'm cutting these impossible boulders with primitive tools and putting them together the way the boss tells me. I'm sweating under this blazing sun, it's backbreaking work, and it's boring me to death!"

The dispatcher quickly backed off and retreated to a second worker. He asked the same question: "What are you doing?"

The worker replied, "I'm shaping these boulders into useable forms, which are then assembled according to the architect's plans. It's hard work and sometimes it gets repetitive, but I earn five francs a week and that supports the wife and kids. It's a job. Could be worse."

Somewhat encouraged, the dispatcher went on to a third worker. "And what are you doing?" he asked.

"Why, can't you see?" said the worker as he lifted his arm to the sky. "I'm building a cathedral!"

Now *that's* the joy of working.

POSITIVE ATTITUDE IN ACTION

1. Avoid pessimists. Misery loves company. Negative thinking poisons the atmosphere. It's dangerous to the spirit as well as to the body. The best way to remain optimistic is to associate with other positive thinkers.

2. Stimulate the production of endorphins in your body by thinking positive thoughts. You'll be surprised how good you feel.

3. Don't be a "grudge collector." Too many people spend too much time every day thinking of past hurts—the time they were passed over for promotion, how office politics messed up a chance for a raise. They imagine vividly in their minds every grudge. Use instead your excellent mind and superior ability to self-image, to create scenes of positive, pleasing emotions.

4. Wake up happy. Optimism is a learned attitude. Start thinking positively early in the day. If the alarm sets your nerves jangling, wake up to music. Avoid listening to the morning news. It's invariably depressing. Listen instead to an all-music radio station or to your favorite tape cassettes on your way to work.

People who know the secret of a positive
attitude realize it's in their power to:

Make Today
The Best Day
Possible.

DAY

4

Dreams

DAY 4

WHEN Steve Cauthen was nine years old, his job was helping his father on the farm. In between pitching hay, he liked jumping on the packed bales, pretending he was on a racehorse. Once when his father said, "Stop daydreaming, boy, and put the bale in the truck," Steven answered, "I will as soon as I win the Belmont Stakes." And this young man who was riding a bale of hay went on to win the Triple Crown at age eighteen. Today Steve Cauthen is one of the most successful jockeys in the world. He is England's foremost jockey now, but he's been riding his dream since he was nine.

When Peggy Lee, the famous torch singer, was a carnival barker, shouting, "Ten throws for a dime," she was really singing in her imagination. She may have been working in a game booth, but she was dreaming about starring on a stage.

And when Menachem Begin, the former Prime Minister of Israel, was in a Polish ghetto after the Nazis invaded, he was raiding garbage cans so he and his family could eat. His dream was simply to survive so that someday he could help his people find independence and freedom.

Dreams are the harbingers of significant accomplishments. Each one of us has a dream, a desire, a longing that represents our soul and our ideal of happiness. That is why *dreaming* is essential to the joy of working.

DREAMS VS. DAYDREAMS

We met a young man who is working in the billing department of a leading business machines corporation, but who dreams of being a famous rock star. Danny E. spends a great deal of his working day fantasizing about performing on stage. But so far, the closest he has gotten to stardom is singing along with the car radio on his way to work.

We tried to find out a little about him:

> *"When you were little, did you entertain in front of people?"*
> *"No."*
> *"Well, when you were in high school, you must have sung in a rock band or put on musical assemblies."*
> *"No."*
> *"So, now that you're working, you probably spend weekends and weeknights at clubs and cabarets where there are singers. You're probably itching to get up on stage with them. Do you know some of the performers in the local pubs?"*
> *"No, not really."*

Danny has dreams, but he's never developed them. Lack of self-esteem keeps him from taking music lessons or auditioning with some of the local rock groups.

So, at twenty-four, Danny is beginning to realize his dream won't work out. His current job as a billing clerk seems to him a symbol of his failed goal and personal unhappiness. No wonder he hates his job.

In order for a daydream to become a reality, it must be linked with action. You must gravitate to the environment of your dreams. Danny, for instance, should be trying to find a job with a record company or in a recording studio. He might even find work behind the scenes at rock concerts.

But because Danny sees himself as a failure, his self-defeating daydreams won't carry him any closer to his dreams than his idle fantasies in a windowless billing office.

OAK TREE IN A FLOWERPOT

Most people are like an oak tree in a flowerpot: they never grow to their potential. The very roots of self-esteem are cramped and compressed by their limited self-talk. People don't look to find ways to make their dreams come true; they list reasons why they wouldn't work out in the first place.

They sabotage their chances for growth and job satisfaction with reasons why they can't be all they could be.

The paradox about daydreaming is that people don't take it seriously. "It's a waste of time." Actually, dreams are powerful reflections of your actual growth potential. As children, we all have fantasies or goals of what we'd like to be when we grow up—a scientist, an astronaut, an international spy, a teacher. Each one of us has the potential to make our dreams a reality. But too often, when we grow up we tend to narrow the possibilities. We say "I can't do this," or "They won't let me do that." And before we know it, our horizons are about as small as a flowerpot, and that's the limit to our growth. The result is feeling stifled, cramped, and unhappy in our work.

BIG DREAMS

Scientists at the Brain Research Institute at the University of California at Los Angeles believe that the creative capacity of the human brain approaches infinity. Your brain can store, combine, and create more bits of information and imagery than thousands of videotape recorders, tens of thousands of computers, and millions of microfilm cartridges. There are no limits other than the self-imposed. So, don't censor your dreams. Give them free rein. Dream about being president of the company, having your own business, achieving great success in your work. The only way to make daydreams work for you is to dream *big*.

A captain of industry once said, "Show me somebody who doesn't dream about the future and I'll show you someone who doesn't know where he's going."

Ten years ago Sandra J. had a dream. Raised on a North Dakota farm, she dreamed of a glamorous future traveling around the world and meeting exciting people. Pretty big dream. Sandra could have whiled away her lunch breaks gazing at travel brochures. Instead, she joined the Army. Sandra trained as a computer specialist and became an officer. Today, she is stationed in Heidelberg, one of Germany's most picturesque towns. She spends her vacations going to the Riviera, Paris, the Swiss Alps, Rome, seeing new places, meeting exciting people, and getting paid for it. She says her life is "like a dream come true."

That's exactly it! Set your dreams on a goal, and once the goal is achieved, it can truthfully be described as a dream come true.

———————◆—◆◉◆—◆———————

We grow great by dreams. All big men are dreamers. They see things in the soft haze of a spring day or in the red fire of a long winter's evening. Some of us let these great dreams die, but others nourish and protect them, nurse them through bad days till they bring them to the sunshine and light which come always to those who sincerely hope that their dreams will come true.

WOODROW WILSON

DREAMS IN ACTION

1. Create dreams that make you feel alive and give you some degree of purpose in your working day.

2. Take a few minutes several times a day to replay your dream. You'll find yourself energized, revitalized, and reinforced in your self-esteem.

3. Read books—they open up your horizons. Biographies and autobiographies of people who have followed their dreams to success can help you forge new dreams and directions to your life.

4. Hold your dreams dear, but also be a doer. Fantasies can only become real through action. Accomplish at least one thing each day that brings you closer to your dream.

Take a few moments each workday to:

Direct Your Dreams To All You Can Be.

DAY

Goal Setting

To get somewhere, you must know where you're going.

Sounds logical, doesn't it? Yet for countless unhappy, unsatisfied people, getting through the day is their only ambition. They float along in their daily lives like driftwood in the ocean. They take whatever job falls their way and exert the least amount of energy possible to get the job done. They focus on lunch breaks, payday, and punching out at five o'clock.

If our goal is to get through the day until we're home again with a beer and the tube, that's what we'll surely achieve. But is that the purpose of our life and work? To quote Peggy Lee, "Is that all there is?"

A crucial component to the joy of working is establishing well-defined life *goals* that reflect what is important to you.

Setting a goal starts with a dream, a desire for something you want. Planning is the road map that leads you to your destination. Motivation is the fuel that will get you there. But first, you have to have a goal. For if you don't know where you're going, then any road will take you there—and it won't really matter what you do with your life. In fact, if you don't clearly know where you are going in your life, you probably won't recognize it when you get there.

THE GOAL-DEN RECIPE FOR SUCCESS

The human mind can be compared to the guidance system of a missile on automatic pilot. Once the target is set, the self-adjusting feedback system constantly monitors the course of its own navigation, making whatever corrections necessary to stay on target. But if it is not specifically set or is too far out of range, the missile will wander erratically until its propulsion system fails or it self-destructs.

The human being behaves in a similar manner. Once a goal is set, the mind constantly monitors self-talk and environmental feedback, both positive and negative, making adjustments along the way in order to score its target. But when the mind is programmed with vague expectations, or the goal is too far out of sight, the individual will wander aimlessly until he gives up in fatigue and frustration or he self-destructs with liquor, drugs, and other sources of immediate sensual gratification.

Your goal should be just out of reach, but not out of sight.

There is a driving mechanism within all of us that moves us ever forward. We can either choose to use our energies to wander about aimlessly, or we can set our efforts toward a target. Whether your job is that of a secretary, engineer, teacher, or executive, it is the conscious choice to direct your energies toward a goal that will make all the difference in your life.

RECIPE FOR SUCCESS

1. Take a dream.
2. Mix it with motivation + action.
3. Add long hours of practice + discipline.

YIELD: Your goal, whatever it may be.

The joy of working comes from the secure feeling that you have the necessary ingredients within you.

AIMLESS LABOR IS LIKE A RUDDERLESS SHIP

Most people resist the idea of goal setting. It seems rigid and un-creative. It's easier just to assume everything will work out in the end, hang loose, *ce sera sera*, whatever will be will be. So most people never set goals. They fill their calendars with excursions and diversions. Rather than concentrate on activities and proj-ects that can help them reach their goal, they just hope for the best and "go with the flow."

No wind blows in favor of a ship without a destination.

There can be little joy in working aimlessly. It's debilitating. Negative attitudes and poor self-esteem fester in the frustration of purposeless labor. Aimless labor is like traveling on a rudder-less ship. You are powerless to propel your vessel toward your port of call.

On the other hand, virtually nothing on earth can stop a per-son with a positive attitude who has his goal clearly in sight.

Aristotle, the Greek philosopher, once devised a formula for success and happiness. "First," he wrote, "have a definite, clear, practical idea—a goal, an objective." Second, he recommended attaining it by whatever means available, whether "wisdom, money, materials, or methods. Third, adjust all your means to that end."

The first step, in achieving success—and we define success as the fulfillment of whatever your dreams may be—is keeping a definite goal in view and steering your actions constantly in that direction.

ESTABLISHING A LIFE GOAL

Whether we realize it or not, most of us have life goals—happiness, a sense of purpose, security, wealth, acceptance by others, health, some measure of success—but these goals remain vague and undefined. We may be busy, we may even be overwhelmed with projects and responsibilities spread out in all directions, but we'll never achieve our goal because the goal was never set.

The secret to productive goal setting is in *establishing a clearly defined goal,* writing it down, and then focusing on it several times a day with words, pictures, and emotions, as if you've already achieved it.

Happiness, wealth, and success are by-products of goal setting; they cannot be the goal themselves.

HOW TO SET YOUR GOALS

On a sheet of paper, write down what would give you the most joy out of your life and work. List as many dreams, desires, and goals as you like. Be specific. The more defined, the better the aim and focus. At the top of the page, write, "I want:". This will avoid meaningless flights of fancy that follow the words "I wish . . ." Here is just a sample:

I want:

to be happy. (What will make me happy?)

to make a lot of money. (By offering what service?)

to be famous. (By excelling in what?)

to be president of the company. (By taking what career steps?)

to own my own business. (In what field?)

to gain financial security. (What dollar amount?)

to retire at 60. (With what income?)

to travel extensively. (Where, when?)

to work close to home. (Blocks or miles?)

to work in my home. (What are the options?)

to have more time for my family. (How will I gain the hours?)

to be respected among my peers. (By what action?)

to become more actively involved in my church. (How?)

to be financially independent. (What investments are available that fit my goals?)

to be self-employed. (What are my talents?)

to have an outdoor job. (What geographic location? All year?)

to have exciting, risk-filled work. (What are the skills, training, preparation required?)

These goals should reflect *your* wants and needs, not what you think you ought to have or what others want from you. You are working toward your enjoyment, not for the enjoyment of others.

The list can be as long as you like. Add on other goals as you think of them.

Next, study your list. Think about how much each item means to you personally. Clearly imagine achieving each one. Consider the consequences of each goal and how it would impact on your life. Which ones come closest to fulfilling your personal idea of a joyful life well spent?

At this stage, you may feel like erasing some goals or adding others.

Now, take a new sheet of paper. On it revise your first list in order of importance. Number each goal and limit yourself to *ten.* Take some time to evaluate the order. As you focus on each item, one to ten, you may find the list should be rearranged. Take as long as you need. A few weeks or even a few months is not too long if you've never attempted something like this before.

Ultimately, you will come to recognize the life goals that mean the most to you.

When you have your goals in order, underline the top three. These are the goals that will most contribute to your joy of working. Rewrite these three major goals on a three-by-five card. Take this card with you everywhere and refer to it often. When faced with a decision, ask yourself whether your choice would help you or hinder you on your way to achieving your paramount life goals. From now on, do only that which brings you closer to your goal.

GOAL SETTING IN ACTION

1. Set goals that are important to you. You'll find more enjoyment in your workday when you are working to improve your own life and that of your family.

2. Congregate with individuals who have already achieved their goals or who are dedicated to goals similar to yours. Avoid associating with people who have the same unresolved problems or who are frustrated by their lack of goal achievements.

3. Aim your goals high. You may not reach the summit of your dream, but you will accomplish much more than if you aimed low.

4. Once you've determined your goal, be persistently positive and consistently active in moving closer to your dream.

People who find pleasure in their work, keep
in mind this truth:

Knowing Your
Destination
Is Half the Journey.

DAY

Planning

JOYFUL workers have a game plan for life. Those few individuals—about one in a hundred people—who rise above the rest of the crowd have developed a most important trait: *Action Planning*.

This is true of all successful people. They know where they are heading day by day—*every* day.

Self-esteem, positive attitudes, and goal setting are important ingredients for a fulfilling career, but in order to achieve your objectives you must develop an action plan.

Success, wealth, and happiness do not evolve accidentally. They are the certain outcome of intelligent planning. Men or women who plan:

1. know where they are going,

2. know what progress they are making along the way, and

3. have a clear concept of their ultimate destination.

Planning is the bridge linking dreams and achievement.

FRIENDS CAN BE YOUR WORST ENEMIES

Care less about the opinions of others. Care more about reaching your goals.

Why do so many people let their dreams die? One of the biggest reasons is *other people*. Ironically, it's not our enemies. Very few of us would allow an enemy to stand in the way of our happiness and success.

The problem is our friends, even our loved ones. If our friends are negative, cynical naysayers constantly pointing out just why we will fail, our friends can literally do us in!

Bob M. is one person we know who let friends influence him. Imagine the scenario: Bob has been offered a new job. He's excited by the opportunity. He'll make more money, do more meaningful work, rise in the new company's ranks. Then his neighbor recites a list of rumors about what's wrong with the new company. Bob's wife is upset that he's leaving before he's fully vested for the pension plan. A co-worker calls him a traitor. Before long, Bob can't think of a single reason why he should leave. He can't even remember being motivated to make something better of himself.

A friend can do more damage than a dozen enemies. Remember, it's easy for someone to tell you what you can't do. But don't listen! It's always the fellow who never gets a merit raise who knows all the reasons why hard, productive work won't get you anywhere. It's the guy who never makes the sales quota who tells you not to bother trying because the boss set the number too high. It's the man who dropped out of college who tells you it's ridiculous to try to earn a B.A. at night while working full time. It's the wage earner who never ran a business who can best describe the fifty obstacles that will keep you from starting your own enterprise. Keep your plans to yourself until you know exactly how you plan to achieve your goal, step by step.

Actively seek out people who have already succeeded. Learn from them what they did and how they did it. If you have a dream, dare to believe it. Say, "I can!" and you *will* be able to achieve almost anything you wish. You can do virtually anything if you think you can. It may not come easily. It may take years of persistent hard work. But nothing in life worth achieving is easy.

Can you do it? *Yes, you can,* but you'll never know unless you try and try again.

MINI-GOALS TOWARD MAXI-SUCCESS

Joy of working begins with a dream, with a desire to change your life for the better. It begins in a haze, an abstract yearning. Slowly, the dream crystallizes into motivation. Then it solidifies into a concrete goal.

But a worthwhile goal cannot be accomplished in one step. Any goal worthy of achieving can be had, but first it must be broken down into a series of little goals. Each smaller goal should lead you, one day at a time, to your larger life goal.

Experience has shown that when people go after one big goal at once, they invariably fail. If you had to swallow a twelve-ounce steak all at once, you'd choke. You have to cut the steak in small pieces, eating one bite at a time.

So it is with planning. Action planning means taking a goal and cutting it up into bite-sized pieces. Each small task or requirement on the way to the ultimate goal becomes a mini-goal in itself. Using this method, the goal becomes manageable. And with the achievement of each mini-goal, you receive reinforcement in the form of positive feedback.

Successful planning takes some brainwork. Start by writing your goal at the top of a sheet of paper in bold capitals. Analyze your goal by breaking it down into steps. Number the steps in the order they must be accomplished. Add on as many steps as seem logical. Break down larger steps into smaller "bites" if necessary.

Don't even think about failure or obstacles. Imagine success with each step on your way. The pleasure this imagination exercise gives you is part of the joy of planning.

Check out each part of the plan step by step. Find out the feasibility of each item by asking authorities, experts, and associates. Research each step along the way.

Seek out criticism and suggestions. You may discover alternate ideas that can lead you to your goal more effectively.

Remain flexible, especially in the early stages of planning. There is no need to rigidly adhere to your original game plan. Revise it as often as is necessary. Even after you've finalized your plan, be prepared to make adjustments. Allow room for the unexpected. Staying flexible allows you to incorporate something new and gives you the freedom to accomplish each step in a better way.

IF YOUR FIRST PLAN FAILS . . .
TRY, TRY AGAIN

Do you know why the majority of people never achieve their goals? First, they fail to plan. Second, if they do plan and the plan fails, they fail to plan again. Too many people give up after the first round. They lack the persistence to hang in there and create a revised game plan. In fact, men and women of accomplishment will tell you that they usually had to come up with several plans until they finally hit on one that worked!

If your first plan flops, pick yourself up, dust yourself off, and start all over again. Just keep in mind that *temporary defeat is not permanent failure.*

Since we only learn from our mistakes, each failure should alert us to the fact that something may be wrong in the plan. An achievement is only as workable as the plans are sound.

In the face of a temporary setback, take the time to reexamine the steps of your game plan. Even a genius cannot succeed without plans that are practical and possible.

There is not a champion alive who has not experienced temporary defeat. There is not a joyful person alive who has not also experienced disappointment. So when it comes—and life being what it is, it will come—accept it philosophically. Rebuild your plans and set sail once again toward your desired goal, no matter what.

Always keep your goal in mind. As David Livingstone, the great explorer, once declared, "I will go anywhere as long as it's forward." Of course, in life this is not always possible. Sometimes we have to take one step back before taking two forward. Sometimes it's best to stop and regroup until circumstances change. But our vision should always be set forward, our instincts honed for advancement. Life is growth, and if we cease to grow or are fearful of change, we will be denied life and happiness.

PLANNING IN ACTION

1. Start a self-development plan. On paper write down the experience you need, the knowledge you'll require, the behavior patterns you will change, the improvements you want in your life and work. Keep your plan updated. Star the items you have achieved and add new ones to the list.

Refer to the list often as a boost to your self-esteem.

2. Begin each workday with the question "What am I going to do today that is the best use of my time and that will lead me a step closer to my goals?" When you plan your day, take a few minutes quietly alone. Refer to your three-by-five card of goals. When faced with a decision, ask yourself, "Does this action substantially help me toward achieving my goals?"

3. Seek out and talk to someone who currently is doing what you want to do most, someone who is doing well at his or her work. Learn everything you can from them. Determine the steps they took to achieve their goals. Note their planning processes, the setbacks, and how he or she overcame negative circumstances.

As any football player knows, if you want
to score a touchdown you have to:

Have a Game Plan.

DAY

7

Perseverance

THERE'S the belief that certain people do everything *right*— that they never make mistakes and their plans never fail. There is the presumption that only if you're perfect, perfect all the time, only then do you have the "right stuff" to succeed.

Nothing could be farther from the truth.

- The greatest quarterbacks complete only six out of 10 passes.
- The best basketball players only make about one-half of their shots.
- Major-league baseball players make first base only forty percent of the time—and that includes walks.
- Top oil companies, even with the consultation of expert geologists, find oil in only one well in ten.
- A successful TV actor is turned down twenty-nine out of thirty times after auditioning for roles in commercials.
- Winners in the stock market make money on only two out of five investments.

It's not enough to plan; it's necessary to *persevere*. Trying once will not do; you've got to try and try again. Success depends on staying power. The lack of perseverance is the reason most people fail in attaining their goals. Persistence is the gold mine of success.

THE BATTING AVERAGE OF LIFE

Not every day can be enjoyable or successful. Sometimes you're going to strike out. But if you keep playing, you'll have your days of singles and doubles. Occasionally you'll hit a home run.

So, too, at work there may be days, weeks, even years of unhappiness and failure. During these times, it's vital to keep your eye on the ball, do the best you can, and stay in the game.

Perseverance does not always mean sticking to the same thing forever. It means giving full concentration and effort to whatever you are doing right now. It means doing the tough things first and looking downstream for gratification and rewards. It means being hungry for more knowledge and progress. It means making more calls, going more miles, establishing new contacts, getting up earlier, and always being on the lookout for a better way of doing what you're doing.

Success doesn't always come to the genius. Happiness is not guaranteed to the most clever. Wealth rarely stems from an unexpected windfall. Hard work, careful planning, and perseverance—these are the characteristics that will prevail.

Perseverance is hanging in there when the odds stack up against you. Perseverance is not complaining, but sustaining.

CLOSET PERFECTIONISTS

Psychiatrists' couches are filled with people who can't bear a moment of failure. Rather than try and endure and maybe succeed or maybe fail, these individuals choose not to try at all. They fear that the slightest setback will topple their exacting standards.

Ironically, these people with their high expectations are not great achievers. But they are very modest. You'll hear them apologetically say, "Oh, I can't do this," "It's not possible for me," "I'll never be that."

What they really are saying is: "I'll never be perfect." *I am not perfect, therefore I am not worth the effort to be the best I can be.*

A healthy, joyful person, closely in touch with reality and himself, knows that absolute perfection one hundred percent of the time is not humanly possible. Occasional failure is a part of life.

To put yourself through emotional anguish over this fact is to waste precious energy that should be directed toward the success and happiness you seek.

You can't go in two directions at once. If you're walking backward to past mistakes, you can't be simultaneously moving forward to future successes.

PERSEVERANCE IS A DIAMOND IN THE ROUGH

There is a story (said to be true) of a diamond prospector in Venezuela. Rafael Solano was one of many impoverished natives and fortune seekers who came to sift through the rocks of a dried riverbed reputed to contain diamonds. No one had any luck. Discouraged and physically exhausted, Rafael decided it was time to give up. He had picked up and examined 999,999 pebbles from the billions of smooth stones lining the riverbed, but none were anything more than common rocks. After months of hard work, he had nothing to show.

But Rafael stooped down one last time, if only to say he personally picked up and inspected one million pebbles.

Out of the pile of pebbles in his hand, he pulled one forth. It seemed heavy, different from the rest. He measured and weighed it. The ratio was too great. Could it be?

It was a diamond!

Harry Winston, the New York jewelry dealer, paid Rafael Solano $200,000 for that diamond in the rough. Cut and polished, the diamond is now known as the Liberator and is considered the largest and purest "found" diamond in the world.

———————◆—●◆●—◆———————

The trouble with most of us is that we stop trying in trying times.

———————◆—●◆●—◆———————

ABE LINCOLN—AN EXAMPLE OF ENDURANCE

Perhaps one of the most dramatic examples in history of perseverance in the face of repeated defeat is in the professional record of Abraham Lincoln.

He lost his job in 1832.

He was defeated for the legislature, also in 1832.

He failed in business in 1833.

He was elected to the legislature in 1834.

He suffered the loss of his sweetheart, who died in 1835.

He suffered a nervous breakdown in 1836.

He was defeated for speaker of the state legislature in 1838.

He was defeated for nomination for Congress in 1843.

He was elected to Congress in 1846.

He lost his renomination for Congress in 1848.

He was rejected for the position of land officer in 1849.

He was defeated for the Senate in 1854.

He was defeated for the nomination for Vice-President of the United States in 1856.

He was defeated again for the Senate in 1858.

Abraham Lincoln was elected President of the United States in 1860.

Never think of defeat as a permanent condition. Instead, view failure only as postponed success. As it did for Lincoln, victory ultimately comes to those who make a habit of persistence.

THE GOLDEN ARCHES

Ray Kroc, who founded the internationally successful McDonald's fast-food chain when he was fifty-two years old, had two favorite slogans.

The first was: "As long as you're green, you're growing; as soon as you're ripe, you start to rot."

His second saying is quoted in his autobiography, appropriately titled *Grinding It Out*:

Press On: Nothing in the world can take the place of persistence. Talent will not; nothing is more common than unsuccessful individuals with talent. Genius will not; the world is full of educated derelicts. Persistence and determination alone are omnipotent.

This sums up why perseverance is such an important key to success. Most everyone wants to be a winner, but few are willing to make the effort to pay the price, to do what's required.

No one is automatically entitled to success, but there is plenty of opportunity in this country to achieve it. Whether an individual worker finds it depends entirely on his or her attitude toward hard work, self-esteem, positive self-talk, intelligent goal setting, and most of all, perseverance. These are the golden arches of success.

PERSEVERANCE IN ACTION

1. Be relentless and persistent in visualizing your ultimate goals and dreams of achievement. Happiness is a learned habit. Constantly practice the principles of self-esteem, self-talk, and positive attitudes when times are tough and your perseverance needs bolstering.

2. Finish what you start. No matter how large or small the task, complete each project before going on to something new. You'll feel the satisfaction of accomplishment, instead of the gnawing feeling of procrastination.

3. Do high-priority work first. Set your priorities on a must-do-now, should-do-soon, and would-like-to-do-when-possible basis. Set them every day.

4. Do more than you are asked and contribute more than is required. Go the extra mile. Remember the joy of working is seeing rainbows in thunderstorms. Don't get discouraged. Hold your course when you believe you're right.

Perseverance in action is practiced when you:

Keep Working
When Others Quit.

DAY

8

Self-discipline

THE true meaning of self-discipline is often misunderstood. Many people interpret self-discipline as self-denial or self-restriction.

Self-discipline, as it relates to the joy of working system, is synonymous with self-determination. Self-discipline is the inner training that develops self-control. Self-discipline is perseverance in action.

People who enjoy their work aren't "just lucky." They made their jobs enjoyable. Unhappy workers didn't plan to do disagreeable work; they just let it happen. Self-determination means you make your own success and happiness. *Self-discipline* is the key.

Many people without self-discipline allow the outcome of their lives to be shaped by fate, luck, or their astrological sign. They think their lives are controlled by the government, inflation, or their heritage.

People who are aware that they exert control over what happens to them in life are able to direct their energies and talents toward achieving success. What they accomplish depends on positive self-talk, constructive dreams, and careful planning. How they achieve their goals is a result of practiced self-discipline.

COBWEBS AND CABLES

Self-discipline is—holding your ground when you'd rather run away.

—counting to ten when you'd rather lash out.

—keeping a smile on your face when you'd rather cave in.

—working hard when you'd rather give up.

No man or woman has ever achieved anything of value who is not self-disciplined. You may be motivated. You may have the right attitude. You may expect to go to the moon. You may even vividly imagine yourself as a space-shuttle astronaut. But you'll never get near the launching pad without persistent self-discipline.

Self-discipline takes guts. It's an ability that doesn't come naturally but must be trained for. The training is mental as well as physical. It may be hard and it may involve change.

Think about it. You have been the way you are for quite some time now. Your actions and reactions reinforce your present self-image daily. Your self-talk justifies "who you are." Your thinking processes and your behavior are crammed with daily habits. Some habits are constructive and positive. Others can be destructive and harmful.

Habits start off as harmless thoughts; they are like flimsy cobwebs with little substance. Then, with practice they grow, thought upon thought, fused with self-talk and attitude until they become like unbreakable steel cables. Habits are attitudes that grow from cobwebs into cables that can either shackle or strengthen our lives.

Self-discipline alone can make a positive habit or break a negative one. Self-discipline alone can effect a permanent change in your self-image and your capacity for joy. Self-discipline coupled with persistence achieves goals.

HARD WORK

We will make no attempt to sugarcoat it: hard work is not fun. Hard work is just that—hard work. Only very rarely is hard work pleasurable.

But self-satisfaction at the completion of a job well-done is pleasurable. It's part and parcel of the joy of working. Mastery over matter, mind, or soul is conducive to well-being and happiness. No mastery can be achieved without hard work. And as we've seen, only achievement with a foundation of hard work brings personal satisfaction.

Why should that be? Wouldn't it be nicer to "get away with it," "have a free lunch"? The problem comes not with the momentary glow of success, but with the creeping worry: "Can I get away with it next time?" or "When will they find out the truth about this project?" You are dependent on the gullibility of others for your happiness.

On the other hand, if you have accomplished your success through hard work and discipline, then you know *through your efforts* you can do it again.

PRACTICE, PRACTICE, PRACTICE!

The young violinist just off the bus at the Port Authority asks a New York policeman for directions.

"Tell me, sir, how do I get to Carnegie Hall?"

"Practice."

You've probably heard it many times: practice makes perfect. Practice, practice, practice. And when you're done practicing, practice some more.

Anyone who has ever achieved anything in life can give credit to practice.

But did you know that everyone subconsciously practices every day? The trouble is that most of us spend our time practicing our bad habits rather than our good ones.

We are relentless in our expertise at becoming accomplished losers.

WARNING!

Losing is habit forming
&
may be dangerous to your
mental & physical health.

Winning stimulates winning. Successful people practice all the time, even if it's in their minds.

In conjunction with the 1984 Olympic Games in Los Angeles, sprinters were tested using sophisticated biofeedback equipment. Medical instruments were attached to the athletes' bodies in such a way that the activity of their muscles was measured and recorded both on and off the track. The results were amazing. When the runners ran the race in their minds, the same muscles were found to contract and expand in the exact sequence as if they were running on the track. By disciplining the mind to run the race, the muscles are being exercised too.

An excellent coach will teach an athlete the correct way to run. The body must practice daily on the track. But some of the best and most disciplined practice in the world is done in the mind. Through the science of biofeedback, we've discovered that the muscles fire to win even when you're running the race in your mind.

Method acting, as Lee Strasberg taught it, is developing the ability to discipline your emotions. Actors who have trained in this method recall, or revisualize, a precise moment when they were angry, sad, or full of joy. They can then recreate this emotion on cue. Master actors do not trust to luck or "inspiration" to do well in a performance. In order to bring their art to the stage night after night, they must become masters of emotional self-discipline.

The same techniques of mental self-discipline apply to the employee and entrepreneur as well as to the actor and athlete.

For example, before a marketing presentation, one successful businessman we know, John H., practices in his mind what he will say and how he will say it. He imagines what some of the obstacles will be. He focuses on the possible objections and questions his clients may have, and rehearses how he will overcome them. He sees himself being relaxed, confident, and in good humor. He sees the client satisfied.

Now, John may have preferred to go bowling the night before his presentation, but he practices self-discipline by staying home to spend a quiet evening rehearsing the day to come.

You can't always practice in person, on the field, in the office, with a client, before the boss. But you can rehearse in your mind. When your mind talks, your body listens.

———————— ◆━◆◇◆━◆ ————————

What we do best or most perfectly is what we have most thoroughly learned by the longest practice, and at length it falls from us without our notice, as a leaf from a tree.

HENRY DAVID THOREAU

———————— ◆━◆◇◆━◆ ————————

SELF-DISCIPLINE IS WITHIN

Positive self-discipline is the ability to practice within. Achievers work and practice to toughen themselves to the task. They know that the trained imagination is the greatest tool in the universe. Like astronauts, athletes, actors, surgeons, executives, and salesmen, they practice flawless techniques in their minds over and over, again and again.

They know that thought begets habit, and they discipline their thoughts to create the habit of superb performance—the mark of a real champion.

Discipline yourself to win. Practice in your imagination. Practice before you go to sleep. Practice after you wake up. Practice in the shower. Practice in the car.

The master seventeenth-century Dutch painter, Rembrandt, once wrote of his secret of self-discipline: "Try to put well in practice what you already know; and in so doing, you will, in good time, discover the hidden things you now inquire about. Practice what you know, and it will help to make clear what now you do not know."

SELF-DISCIPLINE IN ACTION

1. Develop self-control. Don't be a slave to your emotions and impulses—be in charge of your feelings. Individuals who have mastered their emotions through self-discipline are among the most successful workers. They are free to do their job well and are liberated from self-destructive habits that mar the joy of working.

2. Self-esteem, self-knowledge, self-discipline, these

are the three qualities that bring lasting personal success. Develop them, practice them, enjoy them every day of your working life.

3. Your job can't give you anything—only you can take the initiative to give your job what it deserves. Give one hundred percent to your job, your company, your routine, and your service to others.

Self-discipline doesn't have to be a drudge.
Give yourself daily pep talks:

"Of Course I Can Do It! I've Practiced It Mentally A Thousand Times."

DAY

9

Self-expectation

PEOPLE usually get what they expect. Successful workers expect to enjoy their jobs. Unhappy workers expect to face frustration and failure.

One of the most recognizable traits of happy, well-adjusted people is that of positive *self-expectation*. If there's something special about such individuals, it's their overall attitude of personal optimism and enthusiasm. Outstanding leaders in any field of endeavor endure the rigors of perseverance and self-discipline because in the long run, they expect their efforts will pay off.

A survey of great achievers would show that no matter how different their personalities, their work habits, or their chosen occupations, those who have accomplished much in life expected to succeed. They have the ability to picture vividly their success and reassure themselves in the face of all odds that they *will* come through.

Achievers know that life is a self-fulfilling prophecy. Because successful people expect to succeed, they keep their eyes open to new opportunities. Also-rans and other unhappy individuals don't expect to succeed and so they simply don't see or take advantage of a situation. The motto of a low achiever is: If you don't expect too much, you won't be disappointed.

The motto of a joyful worker is: I expect the best of others and of myself.

The amazing truth is that every individual tends to receive what he or she expects in the long run.

EXPECTING TO FAIL?

You cannot rise above the level of your expectation. It's a fact of life. If you don't think you can do anything better or more than what you are currently doing, that's all you will achieve.

God did not put us on this earth so that we might fail. We were born to succeed—each one of us.

But too many browbeat themselves, blame their lack of this or that quality, blame their misfortunes, blame their parents for not having had wealth and position.

It's no good complaining that you don't get the breaks, that people are against you, that you are always unlucky. The reasons for failure have nothing to do with fate or the stars, but with your level of expectation.

All really successful individuals fervently desire and expect to win, no matter what curves life throws at them. Think about Helen Keller, who graduated *magna cum laude* although she had been deaf and blind since infancy. Franklin Delano Roosevelt had polio. The modern artist Matisse created some of his best work when he was nearly blind and aged and bedridden. One of the top-ten marathoners in the world, Patti Catalano, overcame the self-destructive habits of overeating and chain-smoking. In spite of their bloodlines and their handicaps, they expected to do their best. They wanted to achieve and they expected to excel.

Even with a propensity for negative expectations, you may have within yourself an ever greater potential for positive expectations. Do you think you're slated for failure? You might be destined for success. Negative expectations are often nothing more than mirror images of positive dreams. If you already have the power to visualize, you automatically have the power to choose for yourself great expectations.

———————◆—◆•◆—◆———————

Success in life comes not from holding a good hand, but in playing a poor hand well.

———————◆—◆•◆—◆———————

EXPECT TO WIN

Whether you are a manager in a corporation, salesman on the showroom floor, secretary in the office, or an employee on the production line, expect the best of yourself. Your enthusiasm, generated by positive expectations, will energize others, drawing them to you. You'll find your spirits uplifted and your efforts moving more easily toward an ultimate goal.

It's a strange truth, but negative thinking produces "bad luck." Optimistic, positive thoughts seem to generate "good luck."

People who have joy of working believe in the self-fulfilling prophecy. Individuals who enjoy their jobs keep up their momentum by expecting good health, financial gain, good working relationships, new opportunities, and career success.

Optimism. Commitment. Enthusiasm. Purpose. Faith. Hope. These are synonyms for positive self-expectation.

SELF-EXPECTATION IN ACTION

1. Start your day with positive self-talk: "This will be a good day for me." "When I set my mind to it, I usually do well." "I expect to succeed." "To-

day's my chance to do better." "We're going straight to the top!"

2. Turn your dilemmas into opportunities. Examine your most pressing problems on the job. To gain a better perspective, see the solution as if you were advising one of your best friends.

3. Think healthy thoughts. Your daily self-talk will interface with your subconscious to promote better physical health. "I have a healthy and resilient body." "I feel young and energetic." "I am reaching my ideal weight." "Exercise is tuning and toning my muscles."

4. Expect the best from others—that includes your boss, your co-workers, and your subordinates. Be a leader in spreading encouragement and praise. Share your optimism and positive expectations. You'll be surprised how most others will live up to what you expect!

To better enjoy your work and working relationships, remember the motto:

Expect the Best
of Yourself
And of Others Too.

DAY

10

Being Your Best

DAY 10

COMPARED to what we ought to be, we are only half awake," wrote psychologist and philosopher William James over fifty years ago.

Indeed, we all make only small use of our abilities. Various scientists in the field of human potential have estimated that as much as ninety percent of our capabilities lie dormant and unexplored. Some experts say that up to ninety-five percent of our talents and abilities go unused.

Most of us have no idea how many talents we possess. But just imagine what we could accomplish if only we could tap the wealth of our actual potential. A business would fail if it operated at only five or ten percent efficiency. Why should we be satisfied with those same figures when it comes to our work? Yet many of us are. Why? What's keeping us from *being our best?*

First, there's the problem of identifying our abilities. It's not surprising, since most of us were brought up to look at what's wrong with us. As children we're told, "You *can't* do that." In school, tests tell us how many answers we got *wrong.* At work, we are only noticed when we make a *mistake.* No wonder we tend to feel that our abilities are limited.

Second, and at the opposite end of the spectrum, we sometimes tend to overestimate our abilities. It's not that we couldn't ultimately achieve a set goal; it's that we attempt to do it without *preparation* and without *persistence.*

Third, and most importantly, we overlook precious talents altogether. Early in life, we tend to pigeonhole ourselves. We recognize one or two abilities and never look beyond that. There are people who devote years to developing that one talent, and then something happens. A skilled laborer is replaced by a robot. A middle-aged secretary is told she must learn to run a word processor. An executive with thirty years' experience is fired after a merger. An entrepreneur's business fails when the market inexplicably shifts. Because they suddenly can't use their given area of expertise, should these individuals feel doomed to failure and unhappiness? Not at all, if they acknowledge that success and happiness may lie in another field and that they have the potential to accomplish new goals.

Bill C. was an assembly line worker at a Ford Motor Company plant. The grapevine had it that his division was about to be "fully automated," which boiled down to "humans need not apply." Bill's buddies griped and worried. Most were middle-aged and had assumed they would be on this line till they retired. Bill was in the same sinking boat, but he created his own lifesaver. Before anything was certain, Bill took a night course in computer hardware. He let his foreman be aware of it. About a year later, the ax fell. One hundred and ten workers were laid off, replaced by robots. Pink slip stuffed in his pocket, Bill asked to speak to the foreman. "You know, you'll probably need someone to keep the new machinery in top shape. And it's probably a good idea to have someone who knows the line and what needs to get done." The foreman agreed and put a bid in for Bill. He got the job, a new title, and a raise. Bill is one of those special individuals who does his best to expand the talents he has.

DAY 10

THE FIVE TALENTS

The Bible tells a story about making good use of your talents. Now, a "talent" was an ancient unit of money, but the parable has its power precisely because a "talent" is a symbol of the wealth of each individual's abilities.

In the story, the master of a great estate entrusted three of his servants with some of his wealth. To the first servant, he gave five talents. To the second, two talents. And to the third, he gave one talent. The master told them to cherish and utilize to the fullest what they had been given. In one year's time, he would ask to see how they'd done.

The first man invested the money in various business ventures. The second man purchased materials to manufacture goods to sell. The third man took his talent and buried it underneath a bush.

When the year was over, the first servant had doubled his talents. The master was well pleased. The second servant also doubled his talents, and the master was equally pleased. He then turned to the third servant. "What have you done with your talent?"

The servant exclaimed, "I was afraid to misuse the talent, so I carefully hid it. Here it is! I am now giving it back to you in the same condition as when you gave it to me."

The master was furious. "Thou wicked and slothful servant! How dare you not use the gifts that I gave you!"

To bury our talents is to waste them. No matter how much we are given—whether by genetics, parentage, circumstance, or whatever—God is pleased when we use our gifts to their fullest.

THE RUT OF "AVERAGE"

We are living in a society where "average" is enough. Workers punch in at nine o'clock and begin their countdown to five. For managers and employees alike, the job is seen as an interruption between weekends. "Don't work too hard" is a popular slogan.

Our Constitution flamed a revolution with the phrase "All men are created equal." This pinnacle of philosophy in action has disintegrated into "all men are entitled to equal results." The guy who buries his talent should have the same income as the man who uses all his abilities to the fullest. Indeed, excellence is almost frowned upon. The employee who works longer and harder, the businessman who assumes all the risks and responsibilities is often ridiculed and resented.

While we don't mind if someone wins a million dollars playing the lottery, we hold ambivalent feelings toward the man who makes a million through his own efforts. It is almost as if he were an irritating reminder of what each of us could be if we had not embraced mediocrity.

BORN WINNERS

Someone receives a promotion, a raise, an important assignment, the corner office. And what do we do? We think enviously, "Some people get all the breaks. They are born winners and I'm not."

Of course, luck or "the breaks" has very little to do with achieving wealth, success, or happiness. There is no such thing as a born winner. Every one of life's winners worked hard and usually long to achieve his goals.

Success is not in the stars. It's in persistent, hard, daily effort.

Success takes preparation, self-discipline, hard work, courage, perseverance, and faith.

Luck = preparation & opportunity

Put your abilities to work. Remember the third servant in the parable: he was condemned not because he used his talent for evil or because he tried and failed, but because he didn't do anything with it at all.

Every day you face work, pitting your abilities against a difficult task or the abilities of others. By doing your best, you are exercising your will, your mind, and your body. As you learn to accomplish certain tasks or master difficult situations, you are building up mental muscle to handle even tougher assignments and greater responsibilities. It's the only way to grow, to utilize your talents to the fullest.

POWS—PRISONERS OF WORK

Our Maker did not give us minds of our own and free wills so that we could be kept under control by others or by the standards of others or to drift aimlessly without a sense of purpose and direction. We must control and use our talents to their fullest in ways that each one of us sees best. To do otherwise is to waste our lives.

Prisoners of war, captives in concentration camps, the slaves in Siberia know too well the banality of waste: an abundant human life reduced to mere existence, denied every right to make use of its talents. Yet, so many of us in our free society are prisoners: *Prisoners Of Work.* We conform to low standards, we limit

[82]

our growth, we erect our own prisons of mediocrity. Executives clamor for "the golden handcuffs" that will keep them in their gilded cages of mediocrity. Laborers go on strike for contracts that bind them to low productivity. Office workers oppose anything that upsets their status quo.

Mankind is not made to be handcuffed. We are not designed to follow, but to achieve, to strive, to build. Imagination is the key.

In his classic self-help book *Think & Grow Rich*, Napoleon Hill writes, "Whatever the mind of man can conceive and believe, he can achieve." The great thing about the human mind is that once it is programmed for a certain expectation, it will propel all action and behavior to fulfill that expectation.

IMAGINEERING

When we fail to use our imagination at work, our job becomes routine. Routine leads to the rut of mediocrity. Mediocrity is the farthest point possible from creativity, expanding your skills, finding your best. Imagination discovers possibilities where there were none before.

The Aluminum Company of America coined a wonderful word, "imagineering." It means letting your imagination soar and then engineering it to make it happen.

There is not a solid achievement that did not begin in someone's imagination first. The wheel was invented when a caveman thought it might be easier to roll an object rather than drag it. Guttenberg imagined a machine that would mechanically turn out many printed pages at one time. The great cathedrals of Europe were built because people imagined buildings soaring to the heavens. From one step to another, imagination has preceded progress, leading mankind to greater and greater achievements.

Imagination has produced every article of clothing we wear, every bite of food we eat. It has made for the betterment of human life, giving us everything from improved communications to creature comforts.

Imagination is the priceless ingredient of every moral, medical, social, technological, scientific, industrial, cultural, and personal advance. Value your imagination. Utilize it to create a happier, more fulfilling life for yourself.

DO YOUR BEST

No matter what you do, what position you occupy, give it your best effort because *you are worth your best effort.*

Don't be like the man who says, "This job is not worthy of me. I'm too good to be doing this." In his contempt for his current means of employment, he refuses to do his best. He is dissatisfied, restless, and unhappy. And he lets everyone know about it. Ultimately he'll lose this job. Understand this: He didn't fail his job; the job is still there and being done by someone else. He failed himself.

There is no job too unworthy to do well. As they say in show business, "There are no small parts, only small actors."

Lisa G. is an example of a great actor in a small part. She came to New York City fresh out of college, looking for a job in publishing. No one was hiring. Finally, economic necessity made her take a job as a waitress in a coffee shop.

Undaunted, she did her best. She acted professionally and always greeted each person with a smile. Several months later, a regular customer said to her, "I bet you aren't a waitress all the time. What else do you do?"

"Well," she replied, "I'd like to become an editor. So I'm

working evenings here and going out on job interviews during the day."

As it turned out, the man was a prominent literary agent who needed a bright young assistant. He arranged for her to have an interview and she got the job. She was on her way.

Lisa put into practice the principle of "doing your best." She instinctively knew that her waitressing position was not a stumbling block but a steppingstone. In this case it was a far more direct steppingstone than she had imagined.

———————◆•◆•◆————————

It's not so much what the job gives you.
        It's what you bring to the job.

———————◆•◆•◆————————

Your abilities, like your muscles, are strengthened through exercise. If you fail to use what you have, your abilities will atrophy.

God never puts anyone in a place too small to grow. Only we do that to ourselves. Wherever you may be—in an office, behind a luncheonette counter, at a teacher's desk, in a kitchen, on an assembly line—do your job to the best of your abilities. You'll expand your talents by using them. And you'll find personal growth toward even greater success and happiness.

BEING YOUR BEST IN ACTION

1. Identify your abilities. Sit down with a sheet of paper and list everything you're good at. Take everything into account. What talents do you possess? What are your strong points? What do

you like doing? Talk to a friend, a clergyman, or a vocational counselor. Take a vocational guidance test to help reveal your potential. Learn what your assets are. You'll be surprised how many you have.

2. Do a feasibility test. Of all your abilities, which are most suited to further development? Does your goal lie in the range of practical possibility? If not, check out your many other assets. Consider the abilities that you bring to your hobbies and pleasurable pursuits.

3. Discipline your abilities for maximum purpose. Give your talent plenty of patience, practice, and preparation. Only then can you use your abilities to their fullest.

4. Discover a sense of purpose. It's been said that the most glowing successes are but the reflections of an inner fire. Knowing why you want what you want makes all the difference between success and failure, happiness and unhappiness, joy and frustration.

The late Lila Acheson Wallace, co-founder of *Reader's Digest*, had one simple creed:

"Do Your Best."

DAY

Achievement

Wʜᴀᴛ's the recipe for successful achievement?

1. Enjoy your work.
2. Do your best.
3. Develop good working relationships.
4. Be open to opportunities.

Fulfill these four requirements and you'll be on the road to achieving success, wealth, and happiness.

The old idea that you can only be a real achiever at the expense of others has nothing to do with the joy of working. True achievement is actually based on self-esteem, self-discipline, and self-reliance. When you achieve something of worth, you are adding richness not only to yourself, but to the whole world. That's why each one of us should strive for achievement—it's the basis of all our wealth.

The greatest achievements are those that benefit others.

Some people have a strong need to achieve, to be number one. A few are so single-minded in their goal, they neglect other ingredients essential to success and happiness.

Most of us, though, have conflicting feelings about achieving success, wealth, and happiness. It is these conflicts that keep us on the job treadmill. We keep running, but we never get anywhere.

We don't like our job. We do as little as possible to get by. Our relationships are with those who agree with us rather than achieve with us. And a long time ago we decided we've achieved just about all we were capable of.

Why?

A major reason is the lack of self-esteem. Our perception of ourselves—that is, our self-image—is usually so colored by the fear of failure and early learned inhibitions that most of us have no idea of the real *potential* we actually do possess to achieve our goals.

ROADBLOCKS TO ACHIEVEMENT

Why do we allow our vast resources to remain virtually untapped? Why aren't we more creative, inventive, successful? What is keeping us from achieving all that we can?

Laziness, to be sure, is one mental roadblock. Its self-defeating self-talk is: "Why bother?"

Fear is another big block toward achievement: "It's too risky for me!"

But it isn't just fear of failure that holds us back. Just as often it's fear of success. Because we can't see our potential, we're beaten from the start. We make the excuse: "It's not worth the effort to succeed."

Low self-image results from negative attitudes. In fact, negative self-esteem is perhaps the major energy block preventing the release of full human achievement. We think, "I'm not worth the effort."

WATCH OUT! THINGS ARE GOING TOO WELL!

We often pull ourselves down. As soon as things start going well, we begin to think, "I have a feeling something bad is going to happen."

Colleen was a homemaker who found a job as a receptionist at a dentist's office. At first she was thrilled. Colleen had not been part of the work force for over ten years, yet she was hired over dozens of other applicants. But as the days passed, she felt increasingly uneasy. "This job came too easily," she thought. "Something bad is going to happen."

Two weeks later her son broke his kneecap playing ball after school. "I knew something like this would happen," she told herself. Feeling relieved that her worst fears were confirmed, she quit her job to take care of her son.

Then there was John, a low-level manager in a large manufacturing plant. He was finally given a promotion. He felt he had achieved his goal: to become one of the "big boys." But he felt edgy, suspicious, as if he really didn't deserve his success and that it would be taken from him. Not too long afterward, he got into an argument with his supervisor. John went far out of line, shouting and hurling expletives. The next day, John was fired. "In a way," he said, "I knew I would be. Good things never last."

Colleen and John will never achieve anything beyond a subsistence level. It's not that they don't have the ability or the motivation. It's because they don't think they are worthy of success.

THE OTHER SIDE OF THE COIN

It's been said there are only two sources of misery: one is never achieving your dreams. The other is achieving them.

It's amazing how many "successful," status-conscious people are miserably unhappy. They set their sights on one goal. Against all obstacles, they pursue that goal, often blinded to others around them. They step on the emotional toes of co-workers, subordinates, spouse, children, friends, and family. Further, they never take the time to understand what achieving means for them.

So, once they attain their goals, they find them empty. Because they neglected to build a network of support from family and fellow workers, they feel isolated. They complain, "It's lonely at the top." The rigid single-mindedness of achieving success can deplete a man's soul, leaving him disillusioned and without hope.

Self-achievement is no guarantee of self-acceptance.
SYDNEY HARRIS

True achievement is a melding of success, wealth, and self-satisfaction with service to others, rich friendships, and the ability to enjoy all the bounties of this life.

THE GREATEST ACHIEVEMENT

We are not all cut out to be straight A students or the starring quarterback or the C.E.O. of a company. But we are designed to make the most of what abilities, talents, skills, and intelligence we do possess. The happiest people in the world are those who are working up to their potential.

Perhaps the most splendid achievement of all is the constant striving to surpass yourself.

It is the belief that you can do better, that you want to improve yourself, that you will make the effort to accomplish something worthwhile. Achievement takes effort. And the biggest effort is in working on yourself. Try doing something difficult—it will help you grow. Work to accomplish something just beyond your reach—stretch yourself. Live up to your potential, and you'll find your potential increasing.

Achievement never happens overnight. You won't suddenly be all you can be. But you can do it gradually, step by step, day by day. Don't worry if your steps seem small and unimportant. What is important is that you are accomplishing each step and doing it well. That's the road to bigger things. If you *want* to achieve, if you *work* to achieve, you *will* achieve.

ACHIEVEMENT IN ACTION

1. Carry the affirmative motto: My rewards in life will reflect my service and contribution.

2. Look for truth and speak the truth. Don't let the ads and the fads make you into one of the countless victims of greed and the fringe subcultures. You can't cheat achievement by taking shortcuts or stepping over others. You can't fake achievement with a fancy car or a big house. True achievement can be had only by doing your best and by knowing *you* are worth your best effort.

3. Invest in your own knowledge and skill development. The only real security in life is the kind that is inside each of us. As Ben Franklin wrote,

"If an individual empties his purse into his head, no one can take it from him."

4. Take fifteen precious minutes each day for you alone. Use this time to think about the question: How can I best spend my time toward achieving that which is important to me?

True achievers in all avenues of life know that the joy of working comes from the deeply held belief:

You Are Worth The Effort It Takes To Achieve.

DAY

12

Self-reliance

THERE are times when we feel sorry for ourselves at work. We think, "I was passed over for promotion," or "The boss snapped at me," or "My work is dull."

Many people expect someone to give them job satisfaction. They think they're entitled to it. And in a way they are. Every worker has the *right* and the *ability* to find the joy of working. But is this something you demand from others or is happiness on the job something you achieve for yourself?

You can wait and hope someone else will make you feel good about yourself and your work. But you can *guarantee happiness* if you can give it to yourself.

How do you give yourself joy? There are a wealth of ways. Sometimes it takes a catalyst to jolt you out of your passive state of self-pity.

Dale Carnegie, one of this century's leading teachers in positive thinking and self-confidence, tells an inspiring story in his best-selling book *How to Stop Worrying and Start Living.* Carnegie's good friend and manager, Harold Abbot, once hit rock bottom. He was out of a job, lost all his savings, and was deeply in debt. He certainly had reason to feel sorry for himself.

He was on his way to the bank to borrow money to go to Kansas City to look for a job. He felt hopeless and beaten. He was a man who "lost all my fight and faith." Then, suddenly, he saw coming toward him a man without legs, propelling himself along the street on a wooden skateboard. As he lifted himself up onto the curb, his eyes met Abbot's. With a smile he said, "It's a fine morning, isn't it?"

In that split second, Abbot realized how rich he was. If a man can be happy, cheerful, and confident without legs, he thought, then a man with legs certainly can. His spirits rose. He walked confidently into the bank, got the loan, and a bit later he got a job.

The same sort of thing happened to Anne G., recently divorced and left to raise her two daughters alone. She had found an entry-level secretarial job she felt was beneath her. Sitting in church one Sunday, her mind gnawed at the bones of her unhappiness—her husband had left her, she was in financial straits, she felt humiliated at having to work.

Then during announcements, a man stood up and said that a new community member who was blind needed someone to drive him to the hospital three times a week for dialysis. Anne suddenly snapped back to reality. Here was a man who was blind and had lost his kidney functions. She had her eyesight and was healthy. She felt ashamed of her self-pity. In that split second she vowed she would overcome. She began to enjoy her ability to work productively and learn new skills. Within a year she was appointed as an executive assistant and now manages her own division. She has found fulfillment and a self-reliance she never dreamed possible.

As Schopenhauer put it, "We seldom think of what we have, but always what we lack." It would be a good idea to remember every once in a while an old saying:

DAY 12

I had the blues
Because I had no shoes
Until upon the street
I met a man who had no feet.

Cromwell, the sixteenth-century English religious leader, once wrote, "Think and thank." Take a moment to think of all the things you have to be grateful for, and thank God for all your talents and treasures.

Such a small thing, to spend a few minutes a day to "think and thank." Do it especially when things are going wrong at the job, when you feel like quitting, when you think you're getting nothing out of your eight hours a day. Review in your mind all that you have with your current job. You might be surprised how long your "thank" list is.

LIFE IS A "DO-IT-YOURSELF" KIT

One of the most important components of a joyful life is taking the full responsibility for determining your own behavior and creating your own happiness. What all truly happy people have in common is the philosophy that life is a "do-it-yourself" kit.

Many people prefer not to acknowledge this truth. They want to believe that happiness can be found in drugs or gambling or sex or power. There are people who don't want to create their own joy but want to wait until it's handed to them in the form of luck or fate or the position of the planets. These people who feel that happiness is fickle are more likely to live with depression and doubt. Because they don't believe they are in control of their destiny, they tend to make wrong choices, overlook opportunities, never set attainable goals. They are among the multitude of dissatisfied workers, trudging along in mediocrity.

Self-reliance is the personal quality that can turn a salesman into an entrepreneur, a waiter into a restaurateur, an accountant into a financial director, a secretary into a manager, a middle manager into an executive, an unknown employee into a corporate leader. All of tomorrow's leaders begin today with planning, persistence, perspiration, and, above all, self-reliance.

Family connections, monetary inheritance, genetic good looks, intelligence—none of these advantages can take the place of self-reliance. The power must come from within. The happiest individuals, those who have attained some measure of career success and financial security, are those people who have depended upon themselves.

All individuals are a composite of inborn abilities and self-developed skills. While it's true that God gave us all the parts we have, it is we who must put the parts of the "kit" together. You've been given a wealth of blessings. Believe in yourself—you have what it takes to create the joy of working. Learn to repeat the self-talk, "My happiness depends on me."

You do yourself great harm by thinking that other people or fate or luck will produce personal happiness. The difference between your ultimate success or failure will come from the strength and power within you alone.

———————◆•●◆————————

The man who makes everything that leads to happiness depend upon himself, and not other men, has adopted the very best plan for living happily.

PLATO

———————◆•●●◆————————

SELF-RELIANCE THE HARD WAY

Among the most emotionally wrenching examples of self-reliance are the experiences of American prisoners of war in Vietnam.

DAY 12

What would you do if you were locked up, beaten, deprived of sufficient food and adequate shelter, with no communication to family and loved ones, with no idea whether you would live long enough to be released again to freedom?

A number of our men became deeply depressed and despondent. Some gave in to brainwashing and other emotional manipulations. A few went insane.

But many of them dug down deep to the core of their beings and survived by sheer self-reliance fostered by vivid self-imaging. In solitary confinement, POWs wrote complete novels in their heads, invented math formulas, created new business ventures, communicated by tapping on the walls and pipes in their cells, and recreated Sunday worship services by recalling prayers, psalms, and passages.

For those who feel as if they are POWs—Prisoners Of Work—there is a valuable lesson to be learned. Depend and rely upon yourself. If you feel your job is imprisoning you, if you feel as if your office or work station is a solitary cell, think winning thoughts. You'll discover your inner resources can break through your outer limits. If you become unemployed for any reason, stay "employed" in your mind. Visualize your goals, see yourself attaining the success you want. Take the time to learn new skills to make what you want possible. Unlike prisoners of war, you have the freedom to go out and buy educational books and tape cassettes; you can go to school and attend seminars. There's a world of joy out there—go for it!

SELF-RELIANCE IN ACTION

1. Set your own standards rather than comparing yourself to others. Successful people run their own

races. They know that it's not other people they must compete with, but themselves.

2. Start your improvement plan today. People who never go anywhere in life live by the creed "Someday I'll ———." Successful people know that someday starts right now.

3. Learn to depend upon yourself. Don't rely on other people, a fancy car, a prestigious job title, to make up your self-esteem. When self-respect comes from within, no one can ever take it away from you.

Successful people share the secret:

Your Happiness
Depends on You.

DAY

13

Opportunity

THE great English novelist George Eliot once wrote: "The golden moments in the stream of life rush past us, and we see nothing but sand; the angels come to visit us, and we only know them when they are gone." In twentieth-century American vernacular, "The road to failure is littered with missed opportunities."

In waiting for Luck to come through the front door, we often miss Opportunity entering the back window.

Marjorie S. is one example. She landed a good job at a small manufacturing company. When her supervisor asked her to take on a task outside her job description, however, she refused to do it. Sometime later, a co-worker in another department asked Marjorie if she might be interested in trying her hand there. Again she said no. Marjorie wasn't willing to take on any other assignments until she got a raise and a new title. She didn't recognize the opportunities presented to her. Had she accepted and completed the new tasks successfully, she would have been in an excellent position to ask for more money and a better job title. As it was, management saw her as unmotivated and unwilling to grow.

IS OPPORTUNITY KNOCKING?

We tend to personalize opportunity, much as we do with Lady Luck. Too many of us wait for opportunity to come knocking on our front door.

Well, sorry to disappoint, but opportunity never knocks. You can be waiting for years listening for that knock, but you won't hear it.

The reason is that opportunity is not some living entity out there. Opportunity is in you. *You* are opportunity.

Only you can create opportunity. Only you can develop your capacities to make use of opportunities. Only you can discover opportunities and turn failure and frustration into success and fulfillment.

Some people narrowly define opportunity to mean a business deal or a job advancement. Opportunity actually covers a wide area. Opportunity means finding a way to think positively when everyone else around you is mired in negativism. Opportunity means functioning well under stress. It means rising above petty office politics. Opportunity is freeing yourself from the chains of tension, conflict, and self-doubt. It means discovering self-acceptance, inner peace, and confident joy.

Opportunity is directing yourself to a productive goal, to make something out of the talents and abilities God so abundantly provided you.

- You start recognizing opportunity when you stop tearing yourself down.

- You start discovering opportunity when you stop worrying about what other people think.

- You start using opportunity when you stop imagining how everything could go wrong.

- You start creating opportunity when you stop fretting about past failures.

Remember, *everybody* has occasional setbacks and frustrations. But each one of us also has a wealth of potential and possibilities. Unhappy people focus on what their failures and weaknesses are. Joyful individuals concentrate on their inner strengths and creative powers.

How do you make your own opportunity?

Explore. Invent. Adapt.

Above all, remain open and optimistic.

You'll soon hear opportunity knocking, not at the front door, but within your soul.

OPPORTUNITY INCOGNITO

People fail to recognize opportunity for two major reasons. The first we've already discussed: opportunity doesn't sail in on a ship. *Opportunity comes from within.* The second reason is that opportunity rarely looks like an opportunity. *Often opportunity arrives incognito,* disguised as misfortune, defeat, and rejection.

Consider the case of Edwin C. Barnes. Barnes had a burning desire to become a business associate of the great inventor Thomas A. Edison. Now understand this: Barnes didn't want to work *for* Edison, he wanted to work *with* him.

Well, he managed to get a job at Edison's laboratory in Orange, New Jersey. But it was a far cry from a professional partnership. Barnes was employed as an office worker with a minimum salary.

Months passed with no change in his status or his relationship with Edison. A lesser man would have felt his job was leading him nowhere.

Instead, Barnes stayed on, using his time as a clerk to accomplish three things: 1) He became aware of the office environment, learning what other people did and imagining ways to make work more pleasant and efficient; 2) he took great interest in how other people did their jobs while studying the basics of various job assignments at Edison's plant; and 3) each day he visualized his ultimate goal—to go into business with Edison. Knowing that opportunity was in him, he remained open and optimistic.

Then opportunity emerged, disguised as a sales failure. Mr. Edison had just invented a new office device, called the Edison Dictating Machine. Edison's sales staff, however, didn't believe it would sell. No one but Barnes saw that this difficult-to-sell, awkward-looking machine was an opportunity.

Barnes approached Edison, announcing he'd like to sell the dictating device. As no one else showed any enthusiasm, Edison gave Barnes the chance. And sell that machine Barnes did! He sold it with such success that Edison gave him an exclusive contract to distribute and market the machine throughout America. Barnes succeeded in his goal: he was now working *with* the great Edison.

Pessimists see a problem behind every opportunity. Optimists see an opportunity behind every problem.

OPPORTUNITY—TODAY ONLY!

Too often people shut the door on their own opportunity. They don't know that opportunity exists only in the present.

Tomorrow-type thinking can stop you from ever reaching your goals. Your ship won't come in at some vague moment in the future. No use postponing joy for next week or next year. You have the opportunity now, today, this minute.

Yearning for something magical to happen tomorrow or sometime soon is usually unrealistic and defeatist, especially if you expect somebody else to make it happen for you. Depend on your own resources, your own determination, your own conviction that you deserve to make success happen for yourself.

AMERICA—LAND OF OPPORTUNITY

We who live in this abundant nation often take for granted our greatest wealth: freedom. Yet every citizen of our country enjoys greater freedom of expression, freedom of action, and freedom of opportunity than do citizens of any other nation on the globe.

America is the land of opportunity. America provides all the opportunity to pursue happiness, success, and wealth that any law-abiding person could utilize in a lifetime. And the laws of America insure every person the opportunity to work and the right to keep the fruit of his or her labor.

What certain special-interest groups fail to understand is that freedom is not free. There are no free lunches. People are not entitled to wealth they did not achieve for themselves. The creation of wealth is controlled by natural laws of economics. The system falls apart when too many people get without giving.

So, opportunity is there for the making. All you need to begin is the joy of working. America guarantees you the basic freedom to change jobs, get more education, get better training, start a new business, produce a new product, or offer an improved service. The source of America's opportunity is *freedom*, which allows each individual to try to find success and happiness according to the best of his or her abilities and personal dreams.

OPPORTUNITY VS. OPPORTUNISM

Some people take every opportunity to be opportunistic. They trample over other people on their way to the top. They attempt to enrich themselves by impoverishing others. There is no room for this type of antisocial behavior in the joy of working. Sheer inconsiderate aggression only demonstrates a diminished self-esteem.

Indeed, one of the great opportunities of life is the chance to build self-respect. Without that, all the riches in this world are hollow. To respect others is meaningless unless you first respect yourself. Opportunity won't come by stealing it from others. It can only come from within you.

OPPORTUNITY IS SELF-MADE

Opportunities are everywhere, but only those who are prepared can recognize and use them effectively. If a person is not prepared, he or she simply doesn't see or take advantage of a situation. And remember, opportunity is often disguised as a problem.

Movie mogul Samuel Goldwyn once said, "I think luck is the sense to recognize an opportunity and the ability to take advantage of it. Everyone has bad breaks, but everyone also has opportunities. The man who can smile at his breaks and grab his chances gets on."

Winners don't wait for Lady Luck to come knocking; they know that so-called luck is self-made. The successful worker knows that bad luck is created by negative thinking. Conversely, an attitude of openness and optimism is the surest way to create an upward cycle, which creates the best of luck most of the time.

The joy of opportunity is—

- seeing opportunity in negative situations.

- visualizing in advance the rewards of pursuing the opportunity.

- understanding that setbacks are only temporary inconveniences to making the most out of your opportunity.

OPPORTUNITY IN ACTION

1. Keep an open mind. You never know where an opportunity may be coming from. Listen to others. Meet people. If something does not seem immediately appealing, figure out how it can be turned around into a successful venture.

2. Opportunity exists only in the present. Yesterday is a canceled check. Tomorrow is an IOU. Only today can be traded in for hard cash.

3. Supplement your practical work experience with study of future trends and advancements. Opportunities and promotions await the worker who stays one step ahead of his job. Read trade magazines and business newspapers. Learn about what is happening in your industry. Take courses in computers, word processing, or robotics. These are the keys that will open the doors of opportunity for the average working man and woman.

4. Opportunity is a paradoxical creature. The more you capture, the more comes your way. The less opportunity you hold within your grasp, the more

elusive it becomes. Don't wait for the perfect opportunity to come your way. Latch on to every opportunity. Even if it doesn't work out in the end, you'll find many other chances appearing before you.

Joyful workers know the formula:

Opportunity = Openness + Optimism.

DAY

Adaptability

THERE is one facet of working (and living) that you can count on: change is constant. Every single day there is a shift in the economy—in consumer demand and in the ability to supply that demand. New products and services are being created and others are losing their competitive edge. Power structures shift in offices and manufacturing plants, and technology outpaces delivery capabilities. There is an unquenchable human thirst for something new, something different.

On a smaller scale, change is also constant at the workplace. New tasks must be carried out, different accounts are assigned, the boss makes new demands as he or she responds to the market, an old product line is scrapped, a new one introduced, personnel leave for better positions, new people are hired.

Each time change takes place, the balance of a workplace alters. The change may be subtle or it may be drastic, but *each change offers the chance for an opportunity.*

The answer is to become *adaptable* in order to take advantage of the ever-changing environment.

ADAPTABILITY

DON'T BE A DINOSAUR

Hundreds of thousands of years ago, this planet was populated by dinosaurs the size of which we have not seen since on this earth.

Then something happened. Scientists do not know for certain just what. But within a relatively short amount of time, virtually all the gigantic beasts perished. What scientists do agree on is that whatever happened, the dinosaurs could not adapt to the change.

The dinosaurs of the animal kingdom died out, but there are dinosaurs in industry still trudging along in the late twentieth century. Remember, the ability to adapt is everything.

A classic example of corporate failure to meet changing demands occurred in the mid-seventies when the devastating oil embargo created a consumer need for small cars with high gas mileage. The giant automobile companies in Detroit would not and could not change production concepts and manufacturing practices fast enough to produce small cars with high mileage. An ocean away, Japanese businessmen recognized an opportunity and visualized the unimaginable—Americans scrambling to buy small foreign cars.

As a result, for several years the Japanese dominated the market, and the Detroit dinosaurs almost died out.

There are also worker-dinosaurs. About the time when Japanese cars were taking over the marketplace, many independent car dealers switched from Detroit models to Toyotas, Hondas, and Mazdas. Bill MacI. worked for such a dealership. After nearly twenty years of selling Chryslers, he was an expert. He knew every model, every option, every piston in the motor. When it was announced they would now be selling Toyotas, Bill didn't like the idea at all. He just didn't know how to sell those funny-looking midgets. His negative approach clouded his sales presentation. Bill always seemed to end up saying, "Well, folks, this car is nothing like we used to sell. I couldn't blame you if you decided not to take it." Needless to say, Bill's sales and salary plummeted.

Another salesman on the floor, Jim L., saw that his knowledge of American cars would soon become obsolete. On his own time, he met with representatives of Toyota. He learned all that he could and became convinced these compact cars would make quite an impact. In fact, Jim was instrumental in pursuading his boss they ought to switch. As a result of his enthusiasm and optimism, Jim soon became the best salesman on the floor. Furthermore, his initiative so impressed the owner, Jim was ultimately asked to become a partner.

Economists recognize the rule of natural selection in the marketplace. It applies to companies and individuals alike: if you do not stay fit and relevant, you will not survive.

As workers, we shouldn't be like the dinosaurs—unable to adapt to new environments. There are dozens of creative opportunities out there, chances to get new skills, to enhance education, to take on a new job, to start a new business, but often we don't see them. We don't even try to look for them. It is important to open the mind's eye, to see the changes that bring opportunities that can improve our lives. The key is adaptability.

We must cut our coat according to our cloth, and adapt ourselves to changing circumstances.

WILLIAM R. INGE

THE MOUSE AND THE MAZE

Mice, in scientific experiments, are sometimes trained to find their way through a complicated maze. At the end, they receive a chunk of cheese.

If the cheese is withheld, the mice will run the maze in the memorized path a few times, but when they realize there is no cheese at the end of a run, they will begin exploring other pathways. Mice quickly adapt to changing circumstances and attempt new ways to get what they want.

Human beings sometimes are not as smart. Often when we have learned a set pattern that brings us rewards, we will continue to follow that same path again and again, long after the "cheese" has been removed.

In a way, human beings behave like bees. If you place several bees in an open-ended bottle and lay the bottle on its side with the base toward a light source, the bees will repeatedly fly to the bottle bottom toward the light. It never occurs to them to reverse gears and try another direction. Being trapped in a bottle is an entirely new situation for them, one their genetic programming is not prepared for. As a result, they are unable to adapt to a changing environment.

Fortunately, we human beings are not preprogrammed. We are blessed with the intelligence to adapt. In fact, scientists conclude that as a species, it is our superior ability to adapt to virtually all environmental conditions that has allowed *Homo sapiens* to emerge as dominant rather than the dinosaurs.

Modern-day dinosaurs-on-the-job tend to be:
— rigid —
— tight —
— unmovable —
— inflexible —

Achievers, on the other hand, are:
+ eager to try a new approach +
+ comfortable with risk +
+ willing to improvise +
+ experimenters +
+ adaptable +

DON'T JUST STAND THERE, DO SOMETHING!

We often allow ourselves to become locked in our present circumstances—even if we are unhappy and really wish to be reaching in new directions. A position may make us miserable, but at least it's familiar. This is true of homemakers, factory workers, office managers, and vice-presidents. We don't see the potential opportunities around us.

Too many of us are paralyzed by fear of failure—failure forecasting limits our looking far enough, thinking *big enough* to see where we can go, how we can fit in.

One of the most important factors to achieving personal success is the willingness to try things out, to experiment, to test new grounds. In fact, this is the only way to learn and to progress: trial and error, trial and error, trial and success. You may make a couple of mistakes, but ultimately you'll find a way.

It's a far better thing to try to succeed and fail than to do nothing and succeed.

Here's another example: Instead of putting bees in a bottle, put in a couple of flies. Turn the bottle so it lies flat with its bottom toward a bright light. Within a few minutes, all the flies will have found their way out. They try all directions—up, down, toward the light, away from the light, often bumping into the glass—but sooner or later, they flutter forth into the neck of the bottle and out the opening.

As Karl Weick of Cornell University explains: "Chaotic action is preferable to orderly inaction."

Winners are people who:

- Try it.
- Change it.
- Do it.

In other words, don't just stand there, do something!

ADAPTABILITY IN ACTION

1. View change as normal. Constantly monitor and evaluate your capacity for change of pace, for flexibility, for new ideas, for surprises, and for rapid adaptability to change.

2. Don't engage in "all or nothing" management. If things don't work out exactly the way you had planned them, salvage the situation as best you can. Don't be like the number-one team that loses one game and thinks the entire season was a total failure.

3. Don't let trifles bother you. If the effort it takes to change the little thing far exceeds its worth, forget it. Learn to live with it. Keep your mind free to concentrate on the big things.

4. Investigate ways to do things more effectively. Invent ways of your own. Innovate by combining old ways and new methods. Adapt to the things you cannot change but must accept.

Successful workers have learned:

The Ability to Adapt
Is Everything.

DAY

15

Motivation

MOTIVATION starts with a sense of *desire*. Motivation begins when you open yourself up to your dreams. Motivation grows when you *really believe it is possible to change your life for the better*. It all depends on desire. When you want something, you become *motivated* to get it.

Motivation is an inner drive, an idea captured in the imagination. Motivation can be harnessed to an intense drive toward a goal. Men and women who are motivated push themselves forward, plow through the inevitable setbacks, heading ever onward to their dreams.

Do you have the necessary qualities? You do if:

1. you enjoy the thrill of achievement,
2. you welcome the challenge to get there,
3. you have an intense desire to change for the better.

Everyone has the power within him or her to get motivated, but some people are afraid to risk going after their dreams. It's a crucial key, however, to the joy of working. Motivation is essential to succeeding in any endeavor you try.

DESIRE MOTIVATION

Some people think that personal motivation is like a sunroof on a car you buy—you can get where you're going just as well with or without it. Actually, motivation is the motor—it's the driving force behind everything an individual does, whether positive or negative, self-enhancing or self-destructive, intentional or unintentional.

Motivation has become an overcommercialized and grossly misunderstood term. External motivators—including pep talks, speeches, rallies, bonuses, contests, incentives, motivational speakers, and even motivational books—have little power until you yourself want to change your life for the better, when you are ready to internalize and accept the message.

Motivation can be learned and developed. It does not have to be inborn. Motivation is not the vanguard of the talented. It has nothing to do with high I.Q. It has very little to do with who your parents are or under what circumstances you were born. Nor do ability, education, or skills count for much. Motivation is an inner drive that keeps you moving ever forward in spite of discouragement, mistakes, and setbacks.

Beyond the fundamental physical and mental motivators in life—survival, hunger, thirst, love, money, pleasure, and faith—there are two powerful emotions that dominate human behavior: fear and desire.

Fear is a powerful negative motivator. Employers and employees alike use fear in the form of threats, power, and punishment in the mistaken idea that it is the fastest way to meet their ends. In reality, fear restricts, inhibits, tightens, panics, forces. It creates stress, anxiety, and hostility. Ultimately, fear scuttles plans and defeats goals.

Desire, on the other hand, is the inner force that propels personal motivation into positive action. It excites and energizes; it encourages enthusiasm and excellence. Desire is the emotion that builds, plans, and achieves goals.

Desire motivation leads to the future, pleasure, and success.

What a wisher lacks and a doer has is MOTIVATION.

MOTIVATION

For many of us, personal motivation is unfocused and diffused. When motivation is not tied to a specific goal, it rapidly disintegrates into inertia. But when motivation becomes focused on a single, well-defined goal, it becomes a powerful force for success and achievement.

Think of motivation as steam. If released into the open atmosphere, steam evaporates and disappears. If steam is trapped in a room, it can make you feel uncomfortably sticky and hot. But harness the steam to an engine, and it can pull a thousand-ton train.

It's the same with motivation. Motivation can escape from you, evaporating into thin air, leaving you feeling unenthusiastic and lethargic. Or motivation can be trapped inside, causing you to be agitated and filled with frustration. But motivation harnessed to a goal can get you to accomplish virtually anything you set your thoughts on.

Motive is meaningless until it is combined with action. That's why we call it motivaction.

———— ◆ ━◉━ ◆ ————

The bywords of a loser are: I wish. . . . A winner says: I will!

———— ◆ ━◉━ ◆ ————

I THINK I CAN, I THINK I CAN. . . .

Motivation + Action = Motivaction.

Motivaction is the formula for achieving your goals.

Now, many people have the first part: motivation. They fit the profile of a motivated person: 1. They enjoy the thrill of achievement. 2. They welcome the struggle necessary to achieve. 3. They have the desire to be more than they are.

But they never put motivation together with *action.*

Why? There's a simple explanation. There is one word that blocks action, that poisons motivation, that smothers any chance for success and happiness. That killer word is *can't.*

So many individuals faced with a crisis or an opportunity react negatively. The first thing that pops into their minds and out of their mouths is "I can't."

> *"We need this report by Thursday."*
> *"Oh, there's no way. I can't."*
> *"Here is the new sales quota."*
> *"But that's impossible. I can't."*
> *"You can be a success!"*
> *"No, not me. I can't."*

———— ◆ ━◉━ ◆ ————

Those who aim low usually hit their target.

———— ◆ ━◉━ ◆ ————

But life need not be lived that way. There is another word, one of the most powerful words in the English language. *Can.* I can.

[127]

It's amazing how many people have turned their lives around by simply saying, "Yes, I can."

The gap between what a person thinks he can achieve and what is in reality possible for him is actually very small. But first he must believe that he can. Almost anyone can do whatever he firmly believes he can do.

"I can" cuts across all lines of work and all endeavors within a chosen profession, whether your ultimate goal is lifting enough weight to pass a firefighter's exam, closing a sale, getting a promotion, earning a Ph.D., making a million dollars, or landing the job in the first place.

"I can" is energizing. Say it to yourself right now: I can. Did you feel a lift, a small surge of well-being? Say it over and over, again and again, a hundred times a day. You'll soon find your enthusiasm spilling over into everything you do at work and at home.

There really are no good uses for the word "can't." But *think you can, believe you can,* and you'll find that *you can indeed!*

MOTIVATION IN ACTION

1. Start using the words "can do" in your daily vocabulary. The truth is, you *can do* most of the assignments and challenges that come your way. "Can't" is another way of saying "won't try."

2. Replace the words "I wish" with "I will." Dwell on things you will do and figure out a way how, rather than focusing on things you wish you would do and rationalizing why not.

3. Become aware of your major life desires. Make a list of five of your most important wants. These·

are the desires that motivate you toward achievement and self-fulfillment. For every one of your goals, make it a habit to repeat again and again, "I want to—I can," "I want to—I can." Your affirmative self-talk is your most powerful motivator.

Work is usually a joy for people who are aware that:

Motivation = Desire + Action.

DAY

16

Responsibility

ONE of the major blocks to job satisfaction is blaming others. It's a trick as old as this earth. After Adam ate of the apple, he quickly pointed at Eve and said, "The woman whom you put here with me made me do it."(Genesis 3:12). Passing the buck is a common practice at work: "It's his fault." "He didn't do that, so I couldn't do this." "This company doesn't appreciate me, so why should I even try?"

The juvenile mind blames others—the boss, his secretary, the company, fate, luck, the stars—anyone and anything but himself. The more mature mind asks, "What is there within me that caused this to happen?" "What did I fail to do?" and ultimately, "What can I do next time to avoid failure and achieve my intention?"

The practice of blaming others prevents us from learning from our mistakes. It's like putting on blinders. If we do not recognize failure for what it is, we can't deal with it. Instead of making changes to improve ourselves, we are caught in a vicious circle of making mistakes, blaming others, not learning, making similar mistakes, and so on.

THE KEY TO MENTAL HEALTH

Do you shrug off personal responsibility whenever you can? Are you afraid of responsibility? Do you think it is a burden you have to drag around, a weight on your shoulders that keeps you from doing what you want? The truth is just the opposite of what you might expect. Current research in biofeedback and meditation have verified that *responsible self-control is the path to mental health.*

All over the country, thousands of people are learning through training and discipline to control brain wave emissions, pulse rate, threshold of pain, and other bodily functions. It is possible to raise body temperatures in order to prevent the onset of migraine headaches, to dilate the arteries to permit a greater flow of blood to the heart, to relax muscles and nerve endings to enhance physical performance.

There are equivalent breakthroughs in psychology, discovered by Abraham Maslow and practiced by Carl Rogers, William Glasser, Viktor Frankl, and other prominent health scientists.

Their theory, which holds great optimism for human growth and potential, is commonly referred to as Responsibility Psychology. Its central tenet is that irresponsibility, valuelessness, and amorality lead to abnormal behavior, neurosis, and mental deterioration.

The treatment for individuals suffering from these symptoms involves no extended Freudian analysis of hidden secrets dredged up from the past. Rather, the treatment focuses on helping patients to realize that they are responsible for their present actions as well as their future behavior.

When the neurotic, unhappy individual begins to assume personal responsibility, he or she is liberated to pursue positive goals without the crutches of self-destructive behavior or decades of dependence on a "shrink."

PLANT A RADISH . . .

The Bible says: "As ye sow, so shall ye reap." The Chinese have the saying "If a man plants melons, he will reap melons, if he sows beans, he will reap beans." In the longest running musical ever, *The Fantasticks*, there is a song that begins: "Plant a radish, get a radish, not a brussels sprout." Good begets good, and evil leads to evil. This is one of the eternal, fundamental truths of the universe. Earl Nightingale, in his radio broadcasts and writings, calls it the Law of Cause and Effect.

What it means is that for every cause, there will be an effect nearly equal in intensity. If we make good use of our minds, skills, and talents, it will result in positive rewards in our outer lives. And if we take the personal responsibility to make the best use of our God-given talents in the time we have, the effects will be an enormous gain in personal happiness, success, and wealth. This is true of everyone's life.

In reality, though, there is scarcely one in a thousand individuals who ever puts his or her time to anywhere near its potential good use. Most of us fritter our lives away, watching the game from the sidelines.

Nor is there any ultimate advantage in taking credit, rewards, or praise from others. Every time you think you can cheat your boss, your employees, your fellow workers, you are only cheating yourself. When you act less than responsibly to others, you are actually cutting into your own opportunities to grow and prosper.

The truly successful individuals—those who have built great financial empires or have accomplished great deeds—are those people who have taken personal responsibility to heart. By being true to themselves and to others, they achieve the ultimate: success, wealth, *and happiness.* In the final analysis, we are the only ones from whom we can steal time, talent, and accomplishment.

When you take responsibility for your thoughts, your work habits, your goals, your life, you'll find you're creating your own horoscope for success. Once you sow the seeds—being true to yourself, taking control, and accepting responsibility—you'll reap a harvest of fulfillment and joy.

RIGHTS AND RESPONSIBILITIES

Every right has its equal responsibility. As our nation's founding fathers wrote in the Declaration of Independence, our fundamental rights—life, liberty, and the pursuit of happiness—are not granted by kings or presidents but are from God. So, too, our fundamental responsibilities—honesty, industry, and the pursuit of justice—are not made up by councils or congresses but are from God.

Indeed, liberty and responsibility go hand in hand. They are two sides of the coin that represents the wealth of our great country. There can be no lasting freedom in our society without individual responsibility. As long as we use our freedom responsibly, we will remain free.

Tragically, many individuals, some supported by special-interest groups, are more concerned with their rights than their responsibilities. Rights without responsibilities are euphemistically called "entitlements."

Motivated by fear, passivity, and greed, more and more people are coming to accept low productivity, shoddy workmanship, and low (or no) moral values as standard.

It is tragic to the American working tradition, but equally tragic to the individual caught up in the false belief that you can get something for nothing.

Yes, you can choose to buck responsibility, but you can't buck the consequences of responsibility. Or as Abraham Lincoln observed, "You can't escape the responsibility of tomorrow by evading it today."

We can choose to evade or abdicate personal responsibility, we can avoid our obligation toward others, but the ultimate outcome will be loss of personal freedom and a life of little joy.

Responsibility liberates us as individuals. It means making the best of what we have—our minds, talents, skills, and developed abilities. Taking responsibility gives us the power to control the direction and outcome of our working lives.

The choice between rights and responsibilities vs. greed and guile is continually being offered. The choice is ours.

YOU ARE RESPONSIBLE FOR YOUR SUCCESS

Except for extreme cases of psychological disturbances based on organic or chemical damage, *the key to mental health and career success is personal responsibility.* People who consistently achieve their goals know they possess the power to take control of their destiny. They accept the knowledge that each of us has one hundred percent responsibility for planting our own radishes.

You make it happen for yourself. Outside events, bodily functions, and emotional reactions are under your control. The essence of the joy of working system is knowing that everything in life is voluntary—and that each of us has many more choices and alternatives than we are willing to consider or that were heretofore thought possible.

Remember, it's not what happens that counts in life, it's *how you take it and what you make of it.* When outside events or other people threaten to rain on your parade, you hold the key to your responses. Don't just stand there getting soaked—open up your umbrella! By accepting responsibility for causing your own effects, you can learn how to respond and adapt to the stresses of work.

So instead of blaming your biorhythm or your boss or big government, *you* take credit for determining, creating, and making your own place in this world.

RESPONSIBILITY IN ACTION

1. The fine men and women of West Point have a motto: "No excuses, sir!" When you make a mistake or fail at an assignment, avoid whining, making excuses, or blaming others. Accept a failure as part of your learning process. Successful people live up to a mistake as simply and easily as they accept praise. Plan, prepare, and present a way to do better next time.

2. Take inventory of the positive images you have of yourself. Write down what you're pleased with. Remember the good things, no matter how big or small, that happened to you in the past month. You are responsible for filling your inner video with those images.

3. Practice the fundamental rules of responsibility in your daily working life: honesty, industry, and pursuit of justice. Be truthful to yourself and others who work for you or for whom you work; work hard in everything you do; strive to be fair in all your business, personal, and working transactions. Since rights and responsibilities go hand in hand, you'll find your life blessed with prosperity and happiness.

[137]

Successful individuals assume responsibility. They have internalized the motto:

The Buck Stops Here.

DAY

Priorities

IT would take a hundred lifetimes to accomplish all we are capable of. However, we are given only this one life-span on earth to do our best and be all we can be.

If we had forever, there would be no need to set goals, plan carefully, choose directions. We could squander our time and still manage to accomplish something, if only by chance. Time, however, is the great ruler in our lives. It's a sobering thought: the clock is always ticking. There are no time outs. No instant replays. Therefore, an important factor in the joy of working is in choosing which avenues will ultimately take us in the direction we want to go.

In other words, we must learn to discover and set *priorities*.

THE PRIORITY SYSTEM IN YOUR BRAIN

Do you know people who are so obsessed with every little detail at work that they never accomplish anything significant? How many of your co-workers are constantly distracted by every little interruption? Have you known bosses and subordinates who are in a constant frenzy putting out fires in their personal and professional lives? Most of us have. They're everywhere in the work world.

What these individuals do not understand is that the mind cannot concentrate on two things simultaneously. By focusing on distractions, they prevent positive priorities from surfacing.

One crucial function of the mind is to filter out unwanted distractions. Once you have consciously decided that a certain goal, thought, task, sound, action, or feeling is a priority for you, your central nervous system is automatically alerted. It then goes to work filtering out unimportant distractions and transmitting information important to achieving your chosen objective.

To illustrate the function of the brain's priority system, imagine you have just been transferred from a small midwestern town to New York City. Your office is smack in the middle of Times Square. Shortly after you arrive on Monday morning, you are convinced you'll never get a lick of work done. Your brain is overloaded with new stimuli: cars honking, police sirens, the rumble of the subway. By five o'clock you have a splitting headache and wish you'd never left Ohio. But within several weeks, an amazing change begins to happen. You are able to concentrate on your work. You carry on a conversation through the wailing of a fire engine fighting its way through traffic.

Then you're sent back to the home office for a couple of days. As you sit at the conference table, you are unnerved by the quiet. You can hear the scratch of a pencil across the paper, bodies shuffling, each cough and throat clearing. The quiet is driving you crazy.

The most fascinating feature of the mind is that you can consciously program it to be on the alert for priority-related inputs. This explains why some people can filter out unimportant distractions, while others are swamped by them.

Consciously decide, every day, what is important to achieving your goals. Your central nervous system responding to your thoughts will begin to prioritize incoming stimuli. Concentrate your attention on where you want to go. Your brain will follow through.

PRIORITIES VS. PROCRASTINATION

Success and procrastination are diametric opposites.

We know this to be true. We know we should "never put off till tomorrow that which you can do today."

But still, most of us do just the reverse, living by the procrastinator's motto: "Never do today what you can put off till tomorrow."

Procrastinators pay a heavy price. The law of cause and effect is ever operative. People who put off till tomorrow live with chronic anxiety. They usually feel fatigued. The undone task nags at them. "I know I should be doing this, I really want to do this, but, well, maybe I'll get it done later." Procrastination doesn't save you time or energy; it depletes you. It's a debilitating and discomforting feeling.

By putting off happiness, success—joy—for some indefinite future time, you are fostering within you negativism, self-doubt, and self-delusion.

Procrastination is self-destructive behavior. It's like over-indulging in alcohol or popping pills or chain-smoking. No one does it to feel bad, but to temporarily relieve deep inner fears.

What are some of the procrastinator's greatest fears?

1. *Fear of Failure.* "I really want to do this, but I'm afraid I won't succeed. So, if I say to myself, I'll do it sometime in the future, then I won't have to face failure in

the present. I can convince myself that I will be a success, but I'm just not ready for it yet."

2. *Fear of Imperfection.* "I want to do this exceptionally well, but I'm afraid it won't be perfect. So, if I put it off until the last minute, then I can justify rushed, incomplete work. I can use the excuse that this is the best that can be done in so little time."

3. *Fear of Inferiority.* "I want to be the best, to be better than the rest, but I'm afraid I'm not good enough. So, if I never do anything, then I can criticize others who are trying. I can tell myself (and everyone else) that if I were to do such and such, *I* would do it much better."

Former United States Senator Samuel I. Hayakawa has astutely observed a central issue in human nature. "The basic purpose of all human activity is the protection, the maintenance, and the enhancement, not of the self, but of the self-concept of self."

Procrastination, then, is a neurotic form of self-defensive behavior.

Do you have a tendency to procrastinate? Here are 12 signals to watch out for.

—Avoiding difficult work situations, hoping that they'll change if you wait long enough.

—Putting off routine or menial tasks such as responding to letters, cleaning your files, organizing your desk.

—Staying with a job or position long after it's stopped being a challenge.

—Being afraid to relocate to another town. Fear of any kind of change or risk.

—Frequently getting sick or having minor accidents when faced with a difficult or unpleasant task.

—Delaying something or doing it so badly that someone else finally does it.

—Avoiding confrontation with others even when you have a legitimate grievance or a just cause.

—Blaming outside forces for your lack of success and happiness.

—Using negativism and criticism to get out of doing something.

—Refusing to get a physical checkup when you suspect something is wrong. Putting off professional help to kick drinking, drug, or smoking habits.

—Using the excuse "It's boring" to avoid full participation in your job.

—Planning but never putting into action your major goals in life.

TIME IS MORE PRECIOUS THAN MONEY

Time is an equal-opportunity employer. Each human being has exactly the same number of hours and minutes every day. Think about it. Rich people can't buy more hours. Scientists can't invent new minutes. You can't save time to spend it on another day.

You can waste time, though. Most people spend hours every day whiling away precious time. How often have you said to yourself, "Where did the day go? I accomplished nothing," or "I can't even remember what I did yesterday." Time is gone and you can never get it back. Staring at the flickering images of a television screen is one of the chief wastes of time, and the average American spends twenty-eight hours a week glued to the tube.

Even so, time is amazingly fair and forgiving. No matter how much time you've wasted in the past, you still have an entire tomorrow. If you've just frittered away an hour procrastinating, you will still be given the next hour to start on priorities.

The only way to gain time is to use it wisely. Successful individuals use each spare moment—the quarter of an hour between meetings, the half-hour bus commute, odd minutes here and there—to *plan, prioritize, and practice.* Success depends upon excellent use of time.

Unsuccessful people talk about "killing time." The man who is killing time is really killing his own chances for success. You've heard it said that "time is money." Joyful individuals know that *time is worth more than money.* Time is the most precious element of human existence.

By the very fact of your being, you are blessed with a wealth of time. Use it—use every golden minute.

TEN TECHNIQUES TO STOP PROCRASTINATING

1. Take five minutes, right now, to identify what you are putting off. Write down all the activities you are delaying.

2. Do one of those tasks right away. Put the energy you've been directing toward excuses into the activity you been avoiding. Action eliminates anxiety.

3. If getting started is the hardest part, set a designated time slot to do the task. For example, set Tuesday morning at eleven. Commit yourself to only fifteen minutes of time. You'll be surprised how quickly a quarter of an hour will pass, and you'll be well on your way to completing the job.

4. Beat boredom by using your mind. At a meeting, think of a challenging question. During lunch and rest breaks, use the time for creative daydreaming and goal setting.

5. Imagine you only have one year to live. What important things would you be doing, how would you be allotting your time to accomplish the most you could? This mental exercise is one method of going after your priorities.

6. Don't worry about perfection. What counts is quality of effort, not perfect results.

7. Avoid using phrases such as "I wish . . . ." "I hope . . ." "Maybe I'll . . . " Instead, say to yourself, "I will!"

8. If what you are putting off involves other people, consult with them. Your reasons for delaying action may be imaginary. The persons involved can give you courage and encouragement to carry out your goals.

9. If you fear the consequences for the action you've been avoiding, ask yourself, "What is the very worst thing that could happen if I did it today?" Chances are that the worst case would be pretty minor indeed.

10. Vividly picture how *free* you will feel once the task is completed. Free from anxiety. Free from debilitating self-doubt. Free from nagging pressure.

THE SECRET OF SETTING PRIORITIES

Most people have a vague idea of what they should get done in a day. Some people will make a list when they are particularly busy or have a tight deadline. But very few people keep up a list of things to do *every day.*

Sounds too regimented? In the busy, pressurized world we live in, it's the only way to get priorities done. And believe it or not, a "To Do" list will *simplify* your life.

Buy a pad of paper. A small spiral-bound notebook will serve you well. Now list the most important tasks that you must do. These might be setting up an appointment, making a telephone call, bringing up points at a meeting, gathering data, exploring the options on a new project, making a decision, getting out correspondence. Be specific. Break down larger, long-term assignments. No need to list routine items. Concentrate on high-priority tasks.

Study your list and assign a number to each activity in order of its importance. Consider whether any of the tasks can be delegated. Some items might be better handled by your immediate supervisor, a subordinate, or a co-worker in another division.

Beginning immediately, start tackling the number-one priority on your list. Stay on it until it's finished. When it's done, cross it off your list and start on number two. Work down the list, crossing off activities when they're completed. At the end of the workday, prepare a new list for tomorrow. Transfer any uncompleted item to the new page, and add on new assignments. Again, assign top priority to the most urgent task and so on down the list. Keep this up every day. You'll be surprised how well it works *and* how much you're accomplishing.

Some people find that they prefer to divide their priority lists into three categories of things to do:

- Immediately.
- Before the day is over.
- When there's time.

You can divide your list into A, B, and C: "Action immediately," "Before too long," and "Can wait." Another possibility is to divide priorities by color—red for "urgent," blue for "before too long," and black for "when there's time."

Realistically speaking, some days you won't be able to finish everything on your list. But you should be able to complete virtually all your top priorities, most of your second activities, and some of the bottom items. If you find you're successfully crossing off all your "when there's time" items and carrying over the same "urgent" items day after day, you know you'll have to reorganize to use your time more wisely.

Whatever your systems are, what counts is that you can clearly see at a glance what tasks are most important to accomplish. The secret to success is *setting priorities*.

PRIORITIES IN ACTION

1. Become aware of what keeps you from completing that which is important to you. It may help to make a list: constant telephone calls, co-workers who come in to chat, tools or research material never in the right place, messy files, disorganized scheduling, cluttered desk. Once you've identified the problems, find a solution for each. Make this action a priority.

2. Buy a pocket week-at-a-glance calendar. Set your activities for each week. Review your schedule

every morning at the start of the workday. Check off accomplishments as they are completed. Priorities are set a day at a time. In this way, you'll find that you are achieving your larger goals.

3. Make a list of five necessary but unpleasant tasks you have been putting off. Estimate how long it will take to do each one. Set aside the time to do them. You needn't complete all five in one day. What is important is starting and finishing each task. Taking immediate action on unpleasant projects not only reduces stress and tension, it frees you to get on with your priorities.

People who set priorities put into practice
the motto:

Don't Wait Till
Tomorrow.
Do It Now.

Risk Taking

To one degree or another, most of us are afraid of making big changes, even if those changes mean gaining something better. Any kind of change involves risk. And too many of us have been taught that risk is a bad thing.

Many people have a negative attitude about taking risks. On the one hand, they realize that it's necessary to risk something in order to bring about a change for the better. But on the other hand, they fear change.

They know that many people have taken enormous risks on their road to success, but they can't imagine doing it themselves. So they resign themselves to an unsatisfying job, unproductive work habits, and unhappy personal relationships. Fear of risk often blocks any possibility for the joy of working.

Most people who fear risk taking fall into two categories: the Icarus Complex and the Ostrich Syndrome.

THE ICARUS COMPLEX

Icarus was the figure in Greek mythology who attempted to fly to the sun with wings of feathers and wax. But as he approached the sun, the heat melted the wax and he crashed back to earth.

This is what happens to many people who take a chance at success. They set their sights far too high, are unrealistic in their plans, and, like Icarus, they get burned. Some people will try again, without learning from their previous mistakes, and get burned again and again. They begin to think, "I try and try, but it never works out for me."

You may have characteristics of the Icarus Complex if you:

—fantasize about new ways to make a million dollars but never follow through.

—never seem to learn from your mistakes.

—consistently manage to lose money at betting games or gambling casinos, but keep playing, hoping for the "big win."

—make snap decisions without first investigating and gathering as much information as possible.

—have a lot of projects cooking, but rarely manage to bring any one of them to a boil.

The Icarus Complex explains why so many people have "permanent potential." They *almost* succeed over and over, having temporary, fleeting gains, then come crashing down to earth.

THE OSTRICH SYNDROME

Those with the Ostrich Syndrome suffer from the opposite problem. They don't want to fly to the sun. They don't even want to look at it. In the face of risk, they prefer to stick their heads in the sand.

You may have symptoms of the Ostrich Syndrome if you:

—rarely test your potential.

—are rarely concerned about your personal and career growth.

—hate taking chances.

—have little responsibility at work.

—prefer not to know when something goes wrong.

It's easy to fall into the patterns of the Ostrich Syndrome. As we grow into adulthood, many of us make decisions that progressively reduce the need to take risks, thereby narrowing our opportunities, limiting our horizons, reducing the input of fresh viewpoints, and sealing off our potential for joy.

We stop our education, freezing our knowledge at whatever level we had when we left school. This, too, predetermines to a great extent our job and associates—and limits how far we can fly.

Just to get by, many of us tend to seek out a little comfort zone, preferring not to move if we don't have to. And when we do, we take the easiest paths of least resistance. It's comfortable in our safe, established hole in the sand.

It's impossible to enjoy working until you can shake off the shackles of apathy and stagnation. Don't be an ostrich—assert your option to choose and assume your rightful role to grow, to change, to take responsible risks.

TOTAL SECURITY IS A RISK TOO

Individuals who fear risk attempt to live cautiously in the safety of familiar routines. But they don't feel joy in their established, old lifestyles—in fact, they feel lethargic, lonely, bored, inadequate, and insecure. They don't quite know what it takes to suc-

ceed, but they firmly know how to avoid failure. Security becomes the major goal in life. And the joy of working—indeed,
the joy of life—is reduced to mere human existence. Being too
careful actually means risking the prospect of happiness and success.

It's easy to hide with habits. "If only . . ." and "Someday I'll
. . ." are two of the most damaging habits.

Have you ever caught yourself saying, "If only I were younger,"
"If only I weren't divorced/married," "If only I hadn't gotten sick,"
"If only I had said this," "If only it weren't for the kids"? Forget
it. "If only" thinking is a dead-end street.

It's just as useless to live in the future dreamworld of "Someday I'll . . ." It's all too common to hear phrases such as "Someday I'll be rich," "Someday I'll go back to school," "Someday I'll
get it all together." "Someday I'll" is just a fantasy island where
no one's wishes come true.

NO PAIN, NO GAIN

Total security is a myth. The only totally secure person is one
who is lying horizontally, with a lily in his hand, six feet under
the ground.

Life is inherently risky. Birth is a risk. Crossing the street is a
risk. Life is full of risks—illness, accidents, tax audits, being fired,
bankruptcy. Life is also filled with risks that lead to joy—good
health, love, a happy family, satisfying work, promotions, financial success, self-fulfillment.

By confining ourselves to the boundaries of safety and famil-
iarity, we limit our chances for joy. Only when we break out of
old habits and routines do we open ourselves up to the bounties
of this life. Otherwise, you might as well be in a coma or a cof-
fin.

What we need is some way to deal with the inevitable tension and stress that accompanies any risk, however large or small.

You know what tension feels like: tightness in the chest, rapid heartbeat, nausea, diarrhea, stiff shoulders and neck, headaches, nervous stomach, emerging panic. It's not always pleasant, but it is necessary.

Happy individuals, whether they are executives, laborers, educators, doctors, nurses, or homemakers, respond positively to stresses in their work arenas. They know what professional athletes know when they are sweating and straining to break their own performance records: no pain, no gain.

Some stress is necessary. Human beings need challenge. A certain amount of pressure is important for achievement. But too much stress, or stress poorly handled, can be harmful to your health.

There are people who always want to feel safe, secure, and accepted. They blot out any unpleasant feeling with tranquilizers and vodka-and-tonics. Risk taking appears so threatening they opt out for a boring, unfulfilled existence.

One key to the joy of working is accepting some risk as a normal part of life. It means learning how much chance taking you feel comfortable with. It means discovering methods to cope with stress.

It's part of the joy of living: in order to lead a fulfilling life, you must accept some risk taking. No pain, no gain.

RATIONAL RISK TAKING

Risk taking is a part of life, so don't spend your life avoiding it. Excessive fear of risks only leads to unhappiness and self-doubt. We are not advocating foolish risks or taking extreme chances.

Getting burned is just as destructive as never trying at all. What we are recommending is rational risk taking.

The means toward rational risk taking are much the same as planning for a goal. You have to break the risk down into careful, intelligent steps.

Every time you want to attempt something new, learn as much as you can about the venture. Explore. Experiment. Talk to others who have done something similar. Analyze how much of your effort will be a blind gamble and how much a calculated chance. Reevaluate along the way. Since stress is a natural by-product of risk, keep in touch with yourself. Dissipate stress by jogging, meditating, taking nature walks, or whatever else works for you.

The purpose of risk taking is to expand your horizons, to be all you can be. Intelligent, rational risk taking will let you feel confident, courageous, and in control. So, keep your mind on your goal, plan carefully for it, and then take the risk. Chances are you'll succeed.

RISK TAKING IN ACTION

1. Gradually get comfortable with the unfamiliar. Break your daily routines. Put your TV set in a closet for a week. Go to work via a different route or use another mode of transporation. Try a new restaurant for lunch. Better yet, take a walk during your lunch break, explore the area around where you work. Talk with and get to know someone new. Investigate other opportunities for employment.

2. Risk taking can be heady stuff. When times get tough, don't take it out on your subordinates, the

kids, your spouse. Learn how to cope without after-work drinks or midafternoon pill popping. Enroll in an ongoing mental and physical fitness program. Learn how to relax using meditation, mind relaxation, or biofeedback techniques. Enjoy nature. Refresh your spirit with God's good earth.

3. Before taking the jump, clearly visualize all the possible outcomes of your risk taking. The worst that can happen is probably not so bad. The best is probably quite probable. Take whatever practical steps you can to eliminate negative factors and then—go for it!

If You Feel Hesitant About Jumping In,
Remember:

The Real Risk Is
Doing Nothing.

DAY

Learning

HAVE you ever been discouraged? Suffered a severe set-back? Disparaged yourself for your own errors? Have you ever tried with all your heart and failed? Has a personal tragedy ever occured in your life? Have you ever been handicapped by illness or injury? Has a major disappointment ever weighed on your soul? Have you ever taken a risk, however necessary, that resulted in disappointment and failure?

None of these should stop you from achieving your ultimate goals or keep you from finding joy in your work. Failure is as much a part of life as risk taking and winning. The greatest successes have usually come only after countless painful failures. As the great playwright and philosopher George Bernard Shaw wrote, "Success covers a multitude of blunders."

The joy of working is about *learning* from mistakes. For if you learn from a failure, you need never again repeat it. Mistakes are not a permanent handicap. Like breaking your leg, the mended bone becomes stronger at the break.

FAILURE IS THE FERTILIZER OF SUCCESS

Overnight success is a myth. Every single human being who has tried to accomplish something worthwhile has failed numerous times first. It takes practice, patience, and persistence to build the experience to succeed. This is true with learning to work a word processor, close a sale, operate heavy machinery, negotiate business transactions, and motivate people. While it is true that success breeds success, it's not necessarily true that failure breeds failure.

Some people say failure is a waste. And it would be if left in your subconscious mind to ferment and rot. Yet farmers use the waste of animals and the mulch of plants to fertilize their crops. So, too, can human failure be used like nature's fertilizer to enrich the soil for planting your seeds of success.

The joy of working means focusing on future successes and forgetting past failures. *Use errors and mistakes as a way to learn*— then dismiss them from your mind.

People who hate their jobs tend to do just the opposite. They destroy their self-confidence by replaying past failures and forgetting all about their past successes. They not only remember failures, they engrave them in their minds with emotion. People who never succeed condemn themselves for every failure. On the other hand, people who enjoy their work in spite of setbacks know that it doesn't matter how many times they have made mistakes. What matters is the concentrated attempt to *learn* from each failure and to improve their performance next time around.

Failures and negatives in our lives should be used only as corrective feedback to get us on target again.

To turn failure into fertilizer:

1. Examine the situation honestly and objectively. Avoid blaming others. Instead, look to yourself for improvement.

2. Analyze just how and why the failure occurred. Plan and practice the necessary steps to correct your performance.

3. Prior to trying again, clearly visualize yourself handling the job/the situation/the client perfectly.

4. Now *bury* any self-defeating memories of the past failure. It's now the fertilizer for your future successes.

5. Attempt the situation anew.

These five steps may have to be repeated several times before you reach your goal to your satisfaction. What is important is that you gain something from each attempt that brings you closer to your goal.

LEARNING FROM CRITICISM

It's difficult to face criticism. Most of us have a horror of being wrong. We were taught as children that making mistakes is bad; it makes us unworthy of love. But we can learn to *act* in spite of our emotions.

After criticism, don't dwell on your feelings of disappointment or injustice or anger. Instead, direct your energies outward to come up with a *definite plan* to overcome the criticism and get back on track. Then share your plan with others affected by your actions. Rather than spending time and energy displacing blame, work together to get the problem solved.

Other times we are too quick to blame ourselves: "It's all my fault." "I can never get anything right." The danger lies, not in accepting blame if it is warranted, but *embracing* blame. Self-talk quickly reverts to "I'm a klutz. I'm a failure." So next time you make the same error. Or you have yourself so convinced of your klutziness, you don't even try again. Paradoxically, failure can actually become comfortable. It's much easier to settle into mindless self-pity than it is to think hard about yourself and how next time you can succeed.

On the other hand, when you are not willing to learn from your mistakes, an enormous coverup operation results. The hidden error will become like a malignancy in your work, your working relationships, and even the company itself (especially if you are in a leadership position). Hiding mistakes is like hiding cancer symptoms—it can lead to the death of the whole organism. If you are responsible, live up to it. Your self-talk should be "This was not worthy of me—next time I'll do better." Or "I failed to consider this factor. In the future I will know to take it into account."

This is what is meant by "learning from your mistakes."

THE ONLY DANGER IN ADVERSITY

There is only one danger that can arise from adversity. Mistaking the mistake for yourself.

If you start identifying yourself with failure, you will become a failure. The axiom "As you think, so you are" is just as powerfully true in reverse.

The young administrator who sees himself as a poor communicator will invariably find that he has trouble motivating others. He then has "proof." An executive assistant who replays images of herself as the high school wallflower will find indeed that she is unpopular at work. These individuals invite rejection. They drive others away with their self-conscious behavior, overbearing attempts for approval, even arrogant or hostile actions toward those they feel threatened by. This is equally true for salesmen, businessmen, doctors, lawyers, or any other professional with shaky self-esteem. Actual experiences tend to "prove" their self-image is correct. Because of this objective "proof," it very seldom occurs to these individuals that their trouble lies in a faulty evaluation of themselves.

TOMORROW IS ANOTHER DAY

Once the sun sets on an athletic competition, it's all over—someone has won, someone has lost. You can't play the game again. But in work, there is always a second chance. To quote Scarlett O'Hara, "Tomorrow is another day." There is always another chance, another opportunity to succeed tomorrow.

Even if you fail utterly, God is still with you. He will give you another chance. He will also teach you through what has happened. What you learn through adversity can be very valuable—if it doesn't sour you and make you bitter.

Very often you can't change the outside circumstance, but you can change your attitude. "Tomorrow the situation may be the same, but I'll be different." Your different attitude might even act as a force to change the situation.

When something goes wrong, don't panic. Don't assume immediately that it can't work. Instead, look at the problem as a short circuit in your electrical circuit diagram. Don't concentrate on what has gone wrong; concentrate on what to *do next*.

LEARN FROM FAILURE AND SUCCESS

As long as you still have breath, there is hope. Simply by surviving whatever misfortune has befallen you, you have shown you are not a loser.

No matter what happens, never regard yourself as a failure. By the same token, prevent negativism from infecting your spirit. Don't fall into the pit of dissatisfaction, becoming morose and sullen or belligerent and hostile. When times get tough, don't be tempted to turn to liquor or pills as a refuge. They ultimately have a depressive effect on the mind. Above all, don't seek out other failures to commiserate with. Misery loves company and your ne'er-do-well companions will want to make sure you stay down in the pit with them.

The man who believes every other man is against him and who in turn is sour and bitter against everybody else has an affliction worse than cancer. Indeed, some medical experts would say that such spiritual degeneration can actually be linked to cancer. But a malignant tumor can be surgically removed. Malignant emotions cannot. Only you have the power to cure your mental condition and bring yourself back to health, wealth, and happiness.

Learn also from your successes. Don't be like the countless confused also-rans who lament, "I did it! But I don't know how." Such individuals can rarely repeat their one-time success, because they have not learned from it.

When you do something well,

1. Understand the elements that came together to create the success. This way you can recreate the situation for future successes.

2. Attempt to find ways to do even better next time around. Make adjustments for any changes in the new circumstance. There is always room for improvement.

3. Prior to trying again, clearly visualize yourself handling the job/situation/client as well as you did before, incor-

porating your adjustments and improvements.

4. Move on to your next success.

Notice that these steps are similar to learning from failure. You see, it's not whether your attempt leads to failure or success; it's what you *learn* from the experience that counts.

There is no shame in failure. If you stumble and fall, remember, it's only a temporary delay on your road to success. In the face of triumph or defeat, keep your focus on the next step. Never look back. Always move forward. Gain something from every endeavor.

Learn this lesson well and you will have a firm grasp on the key to the joy of working.

LEARNING IN ACTION

1. Don't make too much out of your mistakes. They are part of being human. If negative thoughts become obsessive, get a thorough health checkup to determine if there is any organic association. You might consider professional counseling. Concurrently, associate with other joyful workers. They, too, have stories to tell of disastrous mistakes. They can help you overcome your fears.

2. Find the silver lining in every cloud. You can make something good out of almost any situation. Concentrate on the lessons to be learned in even the most trying confrontations.

3. Set your own internal standards, rather than comparing yourself to others. Accept yourself as

you are, but keep upgrading your own standards, lifestyle, behavior, professional accomplishments, and work relationships. If you must take one step backward, make your next two steps forward.

4. Even in the face of failure, use encouraging, affirmative language when you talk to yourself and to others about yourself. The setback is only temporary, but your recorded subsconcious can be permanent.

In the face of errors, failure, or disaster:

Don't Look Back. Focus On What to Do Next.

DAY

20

Enthusiasm

WHETHER you are just getting back up on your horse or galloping away toward your goals of success, you need one vital emotion crucial to the joy of working: *enthusiasm.*

The term "enthusiasm" may sound phony to you. Too reminiscent of high school cheerleaders or corporate pep talks or "Uncle Tom" smiles to please the boss.

True enthusiasm, however, has very little to do with outward exuberance and very much to do with an inner fire.

The word "enthusiasm" stems from the Greek word "enthous," meaning "inspired." And the word "enthous" is derived from an even more ancient Greek word that combines "theos," which means God, and "entos" meaning "within." So, the original use of the term "enthusiasm" literally means "the spirit of God within you."

God, who created all the beauty of this earth and in the heavens, who is the source of all goodness, truth, and love, is the spirit who energizes you, encourages you, enriches you with the fervor to excel yourself. When you come to understand that God's spirit is always within, you'll be surprised by the joy and unbounded enthusiasm you have burning inside you.

THE WINNING SPIRIT

There is not a successful, happy individual who does not have enthusiasm. It is an ingredient absolutely necessary to accomplishing any endeavor competently and efficiently.

Enthusiasm lightens daily work. It's amazing how quickly and effortlessly a task is accomplished when done with enthusiasm.

The beauty of enthusiasm is that it is within every one of us, just as God's spirit is in each of us. Enthusiasm is not dependent on talent or genius or upbringing. In fact, it is enthusiasm that frequently transforms average abilities into extraordinary success. It's that winning spirit that overcomes genetic handicaps and environmental ghettos.

No battle of any importance can be won without enthusiasm.

FATHER JOHN O'BRIAN,
PROFESSOR OF THEOLOGY,
NOTRE DAME UNIVERSITY

ENTHUSIASM EXTINGUISHERS

Without enthusiasm, you cannot finish a task well. If you lose enthusiasm along the way, you'll give up. It's possible to lose enthusiasm for even those things that are most important to you.

We live in cynical times. People blessed with bountiful enthusiasm are often considered naive, unsophisticated, a bit soft in the head.

Those who lose their natural enthusiasm become hardened, cold, and closed to new ideas and new opportunities. This hardness can range from intellectual cynicism to indifference and apathy, to envy and aloofness, to vulgarity and rudeness. You cannot be cynical and enthusiastic at the same time.

Some people say, "I'm exhausted by the daily grind. It takes too much energy to be enthusiastic."

Physicians and psychiatrists now agree that most fatigue is of mental origin rather than physical dysfunction. Boredom, irritability, resentment, frustration, feeling unappreciated, feelings of futility, haste, anxiety, worry, and tension are enthusiasm extinguishers. They snuff out energy, leaving you feelings drained, tired, exhausted.

Pep pills won't pick you up and neither will sleeping twelve hours a night. In fact, what most people fail to understand is that *energy and enthusiasm* go hand in hand.

In order to get energy, you've got to give out enthusiasm. You need to know how to generate enthusiasm from within and then maintain it throughout the workday.

The great accomplishments of man have resulted from the transmission of ideas and enthusiasm.

THOMAS J. WATSON

HOW TO DEVELOP ENTHUSIASM

When everything is going your way, when you've just gotten that promotion, closed a sale, settled a contract, when your goals seem clearly in sight, when you're filled with self-esteem and positive direction, it's very easy to have enthusiasm.

But what do you do on those mornings when you feel down or anxious or afraid? How do you go on after a disastrous failure or when the daily routine begins to numb your mind? Where is

God's spirit then? Should you just forget about enthusiasm and wait for a better day?

Not at all. First, God's spirit is always within you. It's like a pilot light, always burning on low. It's up to you to turn up the flame.

How can you turn on enthusiasm when you feel so lifeless? Motivational experts concur that enthusiasm can be developed from the outside in.

Here are some of the major pointers:

- Smile. Scientists have discovered that the physical act of smiling actually relaxes facial tension while producing a subtle chemical change in your body. So put on a happy face; you'll immediately start feeling better inside.

- Stand up straight, chest out, stomach in, shoulders back. You'll feel a spiritual lift along with your improved posture. Depressed, unconfident, cynical people tend to walk with a marked slump. Their body language tells the world they are losers. Stand tall and let your posture pronounce your success potential.

- Speak in an audible and clear voice. Mumbling apologetically is no way to generate enthusiasm in yourself or anyone else. Put some energy behind your vocal cords and always keep a smile in your voice.

- Make it your first time. When faced with a routine—typing letters, answering the telephone, selling door to door, filling out forms—approach each task as if it were your first time. Each letter, each form is, after all, different. So rather than see the individual assignments as a lump of indistinguishable work, handle each one with a fresh mind. The same applies to a sales presentation. Even if you've pitched the product a thousand times before, it is the first time for your customer. Make it fresh and interesting, as if it were the first time.

- Follow the "as if" principle. When you must do work that is dull or repetitious, do it as if it were interesting. Make a game of your work: try to surpass a self-imposed quota, attempt to do each portion of the task perfectly, discover what personal creativity you can add to the job at hand. Do your work *as if* you really enjoy it, *as if* it were really interesting. An immediate benefit is the ease and rapidity with which you'll accomplish your work. Plus, you'll have a lot more energy at the end of the day to enjoy leisure activities. A secondary benefit may come when your boss or supervisor recognizes what excellent work you are doing and offers you a raise or a promotion. But the most important benefit is that you will feel better about yourself and your work. That renewed spirit will propel you to bigger and better things.

- Give yourself pep talks. Think the right thoughts, and you can make any job more interesting. Inspire yourself with self-talk. Be your own mental coach. Many people do calisthenics or go jogging in the morning. Well, give your mind a workout to stir yourself into action. A little spiritual exercise will keep you in mental shape for a day of energy and enthusiasm.

- If you think "enthusiasm," you'll be enthusiastic. Action follows emotion. As you think, so you'll be. The bottom line is, if you want to be energized with enthusiasm—act enthusiastically!

ENTHUSIASM IN ACTION

1. Be like Johnny Appleseed—spread the seeds of enthusiasm around your place of work. Greet everyone you meet with a smile. Let others know you respect their efforts. Always praise work well-done.

2. Sing a happy song. Sing in the morning when you shower. Sing in your car on the way to work. (You may get some weird stares, but only from sour grumps listening to what's wrong on the morning news.) Happy people sing, and people who sing in their hearts generate more happiness.

3. Use encouraging, affirmative language when you speak about yourself, your work, and those you work with. Above all, smile! Enthusiasm is infectious.

To be infused with optimism and energy,
remember the definition:

Enthusiasm =
God's Spirit Within You.

Communication

O NE of the greatest joys of working is working with other people. Friendships with fellow workers, productive sessions with associates, getting to know new people as customers or clients are the sparks that put enjoyment, enthusiasm, and energy into the workday. The key to good working relationships? *Communication.*

Conversely, nothing diminishes the joy of working more than poor professional relationships. In fact, most unhappiness at work, low productivity, and job turnover is not caused by dissatisfaction with the work itself, but by *people problems:* problems with the boss, with co-workers, with subordinates. Again and again, the major complaint is: "There was a breakdown in communications."

Whether we are conscious of it or not, we are constantly communicating with others. We communicate not only with what we say, but through body language, gesture, eye contact, and touch.

Good communication means clearly expressing your intentions through verbal and nonverbal language. More importantly, good communication means *understanding* what the other person is saying.

Problems in communication, business failures, and strained working relationships are rooted in the inability to understand the other person's point of view.

Managers, executives, and hourly wage earners who have trouble getting along with others share the same destructive self-talk: "If you can't see it my way, there's no point in discussing it. Do what I want or forget it."

On the other hand, those individuals who seem charmed with the ability to motivate, to sell, to energize others are those who say in verbal and body language: "What you think is important to me. Tell me what you want. We can work on it together."

Successful people in all walks of life know the secret: *The greatest communication skill is paying value to others.*

They carry with them the essential attitude toward excellent communication: "I'll make them glad they met me. I'll brighten their day with what I say. I'll make them glad they talked with me." You know you're in the presence of a great communicator when you find yourself thinking, "I enjoy being with this person. I like myself when I'm talking with him/her."

You pay value to others when you let them know that they're important to you. How do you do that? *Listen.* The most important, but most overlooked, key to effective communication is listening.

THE LOST ART

Listening is a lost art with most people. Conversation has basically become the practice of two people taking turns talking. Very few people really listen to the other person. They are too busy thinking about what they are going to say next.

This is particularly true in business transactions. Clear communication is often colored by power plays, one-upmanship, people trying to *impress* rather than *express*.

In our work lives (and our personal lives), how we listen is really far more important than how we talk. More sales would be made, more deals brought to closing, more productivity would be encouraged if we would listen to what others want. It's not always necessary or possible to do what they want, but we must understand what they want if the relationship is to continue.

Nothing ends a transaction more abruptly than showing indifference, boredom, or irritation when someone else is talking. When you don't pay value to another by listening, you are in effect saying, "You are not important to me."

So what happens?

—Reduced productivity. ("I don't count here, so why should I try?")

—Employee turnover. ("Who wants to work in a place where you don't feel valued?")

—Absenteeism. ("I'm just a cog in the wheel—I'm only noticed when I make a mistake.")

—Retaliation. ("He'll only listen when the griping gets loud enough.")

—Lost sales. ("He doesn't seem to understand what I need.")

—Dangling deals. ("I can't get through to him. It's like talking to a brick wall.")

Why do you think people spend fifty dollars an hour for a fifty-minute hour with a psychiatrist? To have someone listen, really listen, to them for a change.

You can profit, too, by listening. You'll profit in success and wealth by taking the time to listen and understand the needs of your industry, your boss, your clients, your employees. You'll profit as well in the friendships, loyalty, and cooperation that others will gladly give you for the simple reason that you paid them value by listening.

ACTIVE LISTENING

A great stage director once said, "Acting is reacting. It's done with the ears, not the mouth."

Contrary to popular belief, listening is not passive, it's active.

How do you get someone's attention? It's not by talking or by making clever remarks or by trying to impress others with yourself. If you want to get people interested in you, talk about what is important to them.

The biggest mistake most people make in communicating is talking about Me, Myself, and I: "What *I* want to sell . . . " "These are *my* needs. . . . " "*I* would like this job because *I* . . ."

Instead, turn your attention to the other person: "What are *your* needs?" "How can I help *you*?" "What can I provide for *you* and *your* company?" Then listen.

Always pivot the conversation around the other person. Talk about people, places, and things that are important to him or her.

It's been said that by showing interest in people you can make more friends in twenty minutes than you can in twenty weeks by showing how interesting you are.

GETTING YOUR MESSAGE ACROSS

Do you ever find yourself in this sort of frustrated rage? "No, no, no. That's not what I wanted!" or "Why can't they ever do what

I ask?" or "I gave perfectly clear instructions but got back some-thing totally different!"

The first thing you must understand is that the problem is not with them but with you. If you are having trouble getting your message across, the problem is most likely *your* difficulty in com-municating.

As simple as it sounds, the first step in getting your message across to others is knowing exactly what it is you want. Too many people express themselves in vague, imprecise language, because they themselves are unclear about their intentions. Take the time to think through your ideas before you leave them open to mis-interpretation.

Second, use plain language spoken in practical terms. If some-one fails to understand you, it's not his or her fault. You are re-sponsible for making certain your concepts are clear. Listen to yourself as you speak. Do *you* understand what you're saying?

Third, ask for feedback—"Does this make sense to you?" "How would you sum it up?" "Could you please give me your interpre-tation of this?" Then listen as your communication is fed back to you. It can be quite a mind-opening experience.

TWELVE TIPS TO BETTER COMMUNICATION

Good communication is the art of projecting ourselves through eye and ear contact. *Look* at another person directly and *listen* with complete attention.

These are the fundamental keys to effective communication. There are a number of other tips and pointers we'd like to share with you. Some of them may sound so obvious they seem silly even to mention. But you'd be surprised how many people never use them at all.

COMMUNICATION

1. Introduce yourself up front. Whether talking in person or on the telephone, lead with your name. "Glad to meet you, my name is _____," or "Hello, this is _____ speaking." Few things are more distracting in the opening moments of a conversation than thinking, "*Who* is this I'm talking to?"

2. Practice developing a good, firm handshake. This applies as equally to women as to men. Take the initiative—extend your hand first.

3. Remember names. It's one of the most important tributes you can pay another person. Pay attention when someone introduces himself. Repeat his name immediately, as in: "David Johnson, I'm glad to know you." If you didn't quite catch the name, say so: "I'm sorry, I didn't quite catch your name." The other person will appreciate your genuine interest in learning his name correctly.

4. Make eye contact when you are speaking. When someone else is talking, look directly in his eyes. Eye contact communicates the confidence you have in what you're saying and shows you are giving value to what the other person is expressing.

5. Adopt the attitude "I'll make her glad she talked with me." Say something good about the other person. Ask questions about her interests. Help draw the other person out. She will be glad she talked with you.

6. Talk positively. A happy outlook is contagious. Share your enjoyment of your work, your day, your life. You'll find people eager to associate with you. By the same token, avoid complaining or griping (even if you feel you have cause). Negativism drags people down. They

have their own troubles—don't burden them with yours.

7. Learn discretion. Not everything someone tells you is meant to be repeated to others. Let people feel confident they can trust you with their confidences.

8. Be service-oriented rather than self-oriented. Show your interest in the other person's concerns, not just your own. When you have someone else's interest at heart, he or she can sense it and will be drawn to you. Conversely, people become uneasy when they sense a person has only his own interests in mind.

9. Make the other person feel important—give him your full attention. Act as if his or her job, problem, or experience is of tantamount importance to you at this moment. Keep the other person's interests in your foreground and you'll be respected as an intelligent, skilled, and caring communicator.

10. Make sure you fully understand what the other person has said. More headaches occur on the job because of misinterpretations and misunderstandings than for any other reason. To be certain you get the other person's meaning, repeat what she's said by putting it in your own words. Ask the other person if you are comprehending her clearly. She'll appreciate being understood and will be impressed with your effort to understand.

11. Be prompt for meetings and appointments. When you arrive late, you are in effect saying, "This is not important to me." If unforeseen circumstances beyond your control cause you to keep others waiting, telephone them. Honestly explain the reason for your delay and estimate when you'll get there. You'll win respect for your consideration instead of consternation for your tardiness.

12. Empathize with others. Try to become more sensitive and open to the needs and differences of others. Try to view the world as others see it. Try seeing yourself as others see you: "How would I like working for me?" "How does my supervisor like my performance?" You will become a far more effective communicator when you understand how you are coming across to others.

In essence, the secret to good communication is to bring that other person over to your side. The most effective way to do this is to make the other person feel valued. Feeling valued, feeling important is probably the most fundamental of human emotional needs. If people are made to feel important, they will reciprocate in kind with openness, cooperation, and mutual respect.

We can't think of a more pleasurable working relationship than one based on openness, cooperation, and mutual respect. So, *communicate* your enthusiasm, your self-esteem, your energy to others. You'll soon find yourself surrounded by people who share your joy of working.

COMMUNICATION IN ACTION

1. Treat people more like brothers and sisters. This includes your boss, co-workers, and subordinates. Pay value to everyone you encounter in your workday. Especially value those people who work for you. You would not be where you are without them.

2. Listen. The greater half of communication is in listening. When someone is talking to you, give him or her your full attention.

[187]

3. When you speak, project constructive, supportive ideas. Be neither cynical nor critical. Accept other viewpoints as being valid even if they are diametrically opposed to your own beliefs.

4. Look at yourself through other people's eyes. Imagine being your boss, the person working next to you, your employee. When you come into an office, what do you think a stranger's first impression of you will be? Why?

The paradoxical secret of good communications is listening. Put another way:

The Greatest
Communication Skill Is
Paying Value to Others.

DAY

22

Cooperation

THE definition of the word "cooperation" stems from two Latin words, "co," meaning "with," and "opus," meaning "work." So, quite literally, cooperation means working with others.

And that's exactly what we do. Whether we are on an assembly line, behind a word processor, or on the phone, we spend eight hours a day *working with others.* Enjoying your relationships with people is a critical factor to liking work. The joy we find in our jobs can be directly related to how well we work with others—in other words, how well we cooperate.

Successful cooperation is a two-way street. You can't expect others to cooperate with you if you don't give an inch. Conversely, you shouldn't feel as if you are the one who is always "cooperative" while others get their own way. Nowhere in the definition of the word does "cooperate" mean "giving in."

No matter how much ability a person has, no matter how intelligent he is, no matter how hard he can work, he will not go far in his career, nor will he enjoy his job, without the cooperation of others. The road to success is paved with cooperative relationships.

CO-WINNING

The joy of working has nothing to do with the manipulate-your-way-to-number-one attitude. There can be little satisfaction in winning career battles at the expense of other human beings. Individuals who *must* be number one usually harbor deep insecurities, carry disdain for others or suffer from compulsive/manic tendencies. In the end, they lose the ball game of life.

It's one of the tragedies of our culture that people feel they must claw their way to the top. Daytime soap operas and prime-time glamour dramas enhance the image of ruthless, self-serving manipulators. But in real life, do-it-to-them-before-they-do-it-to-me is a pathetic philosophy to live by.

People who try to dominate others are desperately attempting to gain external worthiness to make up for internal neurosis.

The losers in life, those who work in joyless compulsion, have the "I win and you lose" attitude. Ultimately, it becomes the "lose-lose" attitude. But winners practice the co-winning attitude: "If I help you win, then I win."

That's the essence of the art of successful cooperation.

Think about the people with whom you work well. You'll likely find they are people you care about—a friend in the office, your secretary, a business associate, your mentor—and these are people who also are interested in you. The people who are most cooperative with you are the people you care about. Cooperation flourishes when other people's interests are uppermost in your mind, not yours.

This is evident in the work arena, but it's also true in most every other area of our lives, including marriage and parenthood. It has been said that "marriage is not looking at each other, but looking out in the same direction together." And this is just as applicable to worker cooperation as it is to a marriage that works well.

[193]

Ten Roadblocks to Cooperation	Ten Bridges to Success
Unreliability	Reliability
Hostility	Goodwill
Laziness	Willingness
Untidiness	Neatness
Suspicion	Openness
Trouble making	Cheerfulness
Controversy	Courtesy
Interference	Trust
Dishonesty	Honesty
Selfishness	Empathy

THE TAKERS

It's interesting to note that the "takers" in life, the ones who never give an inch, who forever find fault, who seem to have impossible egos, are incapable of working well with others because of low self-esteem and low self-image.

What they are really saying is: "I've got to look strong. I have to be superior. I can't let them know how insecure I really am."

People who try to appear overly important and have a reputation for inflexibility may actually be covering up a deep inner fear. Underneath the hard exterior shell is usually a soft, vulnerable person who wants to be dependent on others.

They can't allow that to happen, however, because they will not trust anyone. At some point in their lives they felt hurt and taken advantage of by someone important to them. Therefore they dare not leave themselves open to be hurt and used again. They must always keep their defenses up. To prevent the possibility of injury to their essential soft, vulnerable personae, they preclude any potential for the normal give and take in a relationship. So they become takers.

COOPERATION MEANS COMMUNICATION

Whatever your goal is—to enjoy the workday, to increase your income, or to become chairman of the board—you will need the cooperation of others to reach it. You'll need the pull of the boss above you, the support of those subordinate to you, and the buttressing of your peers and associates around you.

Building this kind of interpersonal structure is one of the best examples of the joy of working.

To get others to lend you their support requires the negotiation keystone: "If I help you win, then I win too." In other words, people must perceive a direct benefit to themselves in helping you do what you want to do. You can't expect others to cooperate if they feel exploited. Attempting to control your work environment at the expense of others will end in failure. Cooperation means working *with* another person, not *for* him.

Most of our working (and personal) relationships operate on two levels: the emotional and the rational.

For example, a fellow worker with whom you are usually friendly ignores you as he passes in the hall. Your first reaction is emotional. You think, "Is Joe angry at me?" or "Now that he got a small promotion, is he snubbing me?" So you speak up first: "Hey, Joe, what's the matter? You're not talking to me?" Joe turns around and smiles at you. His hand reaches out to you. "Mike! I'm sorry, I was so preoccupied with my thoughts, I didn't even see you walk by. How are you doing?" When he explains, you realize you were not being rebuffed and put the matter out of your mind.

Your first response was emotional. You perceived hurt and you reacted defensively. As soon as you received verbal information, the rational part of your mind put the situation in perspective.

The encounter might have gone the other way. Let's say you let Joe pass by. You perceived a slight. So next time he feels a chill. Rather than confront you, he avoids you, confirming your first suspicion. The tension between you grows. Finally, when Joe is in a position to recommend someone for a new assignment, he suggests Betsy. You are furious. The friendship comes to blows, and any future possibility for cooperation is lost.

Emotions often block the possibility for cooperation. Certainly, emotions are important barometers to changes in interpersonal working relationships. We should stay attuned to the feelings of our boss, our co-workers, those who work for us. But emotions, particularly those emotions strongly felt, should be further explored through open communications with the other person involved. Our immediate feelings should be tempered through logic and common sense. Business partnerships and other work relationships would be stronger, more productive, and more satisfying if there was more communication on the job. The same can be said for marriage and every other cooperative venture.

Of course, no relationship is ever one hundred percent perfect. The very nature of human interaction is that it is in a constant state of flux.

The goal in successful cooperation is to *improve* the relationships with all your co-workers and associates. Take the initiative. Speak up first. Keep the lines of communication open.

I, ME, MINE

Do you know what's the most popular word in the English language? You've guessed it—it's the personal pronoun "I." "I" is the most frequently occurring word in spoken conversation. Coming in for a close second, third, and fourth are "me," "my," and "mine."

"You" and "yours" aren't even in the top twenty.

"I" am so involved with "me" that there's no room for "you." No wonder cooperation, which involves "you" and "me," so often falls apart. The cult of the "self" is pervasive. Alfred Adler, the renowned psychologist, confirms the void of the self-oriented person:

It is the individual who is not interested in his fellow men who has the greatest difficulties in life and provides the greatest injury to others. It is from among such individuals that all human failures spring.

It is the person who actively cultivates an interest in other people who brings joy into his own life and into the workplace. Once again, the eternal law of cause and effect is at work. *When you show interest in others, they will begin to be interested in you.* It's a happy boomerang effect. By becoming genuinely interested in others, you'll soon find yourself surrounded by friends at work who enjoy cooperating and working with you.

HOW TO GET ENTHUSIASTIC COOPERATION

It was a sticky ninety-five degrees outside when Ronnie L. whirled through the revolving doors of the central TWA ticket office in midtown Manhattan. The bright red reception room was crowded with travelers. Like the others, Ronnie waited in line. She stood behind a chain-smoking, somewhat overweight man who appeared agitated with the long wait. When it finally was his turn, the whole travel office could hear the exchange. He was in a hurry, he barked. He wanted *this* flight *now.* Why was the price so high? What did she mean first class was sold out? And on and on. The poor woman behind the counter looked as if she could strangle him and burst into tears at the same time.

At last, the man stomped off and it was Ronnie's turn. Ronnie needed to arrange a rather complex flight schedule with several stopovers, but wanted to find the least expensive connections. She knew this would take some time and effort on the part of the reservations clerk.

Ronnie paused for a moment in front of the counter. The clerk didn't even look up; she was still sorting through the jumble of paperwork from the last customer. "Yes?" she said curtly.

"You look as though you've had a very tiring day," Ronnie replied.

The clerk looked up at her. This was the first time someone had actually paid attention to her as a human being rather than as an extension of a computer. "Why, yes, I have. We've been swamped with people. It's the tourist season, you know. And I've got a cold, I feel really miserable, and the air conditioning in here is freezing."

Ronnie commiserated with the clerk, saying that it was awful to have a cold in the summer. "In spite of all that, you seem to be handling the situation really well. That last customer you had was particularly difficult, but you dealt with him very professionally. That's a great skill to have."

Now the clerk was smiling broadly. "Oh, he wasn't so bad. We all try to do a good job. Now, how can I help you?"

Ronnie got the flights she wanted and the lowest possible fares. But she got much more than that. She got a surge of joy. There is no better feeling on this earth than to give a little of yourself to brighten another person's day.

The clerk also felt rewarded. She was appreciated for her work by a customer. Suddenly, her cold seemed better, and the crowd easier to bear. It was going to be a good day after all. She, too, got the joy. That's co-winning in action. *If I help you win, I win too.*

How can you get enthusiastic cooperation from others? It's easy—*you'll get back in direct proportion to what you give.*

- Pay value to the other person. Show him that his feelings count.

- Make the other person feel important. Respect her individuality.

- Find something nice to say. Let the other person feel at ease with you.

- Listen—give the other person your full attention.

- Empathize with him. Try to understand what it would be like in his shoes.

- Give of yourself. You'll find you'll get much more in return.

COOPERATION IN ACTION

1. Carry the affirmative motto: "My rewards in life will reflect my service and contribution in every daily transaction."

2. Make a contribution to something or someone for which there is no direct payoff or obligation.

3. Project positive self-esteem. Get that deep-down feeling of your own worth and pass it along to others. Talk yourself and others up.

4. Practice positive self-expectancy. Put another's interests ahead of yours and go into the situation with a positive feeling that he or she will do the same. "Goodwill" expectations are amazingly contagious. If you think "cooperation," you will almost always achieve it.

The joy of working *with* others lies in its definition:

Cooperation
Is a Two-Letter Word—
WE.

DAY

23

Negotiation

THERE'S a reason why so many people have trepidation about negotiating, and that's because they really don't know how to negotiate. Negotiation experts say it is an art. But the art of negotiating is not just for international diplomats, nor do you have to be tough as nails to negotiate well.

In fact, skilled negotiators—businessmen, lawyers, transactional psychologists—agree that the basis of successful negotiation lies in the ability to understand clearly what the other person wants, as well as to express effectively your needs.

Negotiation is a means to discuss, to communicate, to interact with another human being in order to find a way to reach an agreement.

The art of negotiation is an attitude to be adopted as much as it is a skill to be learned. Negotiating well, with a satisfying outcome for all people involved, is part of the joy of working.

SEE IT THEIR WAY

Bullies make poor negotiators. That applies to verbal bullies as well as physical ones. Contrary to popular belief, no one wins by

intimidation. It only makes the other person defensive and re-
sentful.

The rules to successful negotiation are based on the principles
of communication and cooperation. First, you want the other
person to talk with you and, second, you want him to work with
you. In other words, negotiation is the gentle art of persuading
the other fellow that you can help him achieve his goals if he
helps you achieve yours.

You have a much greater chance of successfully negotiating a
situation if you first understand the point of view of the other
person involved. Put yourself in his shoes. Let him know that
you value his perspective. You'll be in a far better position to
win him over to your side.

Before a negotiation encounter, anticipate the points the other
person will bring up. What might he say about you, your work,
your request? Mentally rehearse the encounter, taking both sides
in the discussion. Follow this sage advice offered by Abraham
Lincoln: "When I'm getting ready to reason with a man, I spend
one-third of my time thinking about myself and what I'm going
to say—and two-thirds thinking about him and what he is going
to say."

If you must counter or criticize, do so constructively. Never
try to bully or intimidate the other person. He'll be that much
more reluctant to join forces in your camp.

During the actual negotiation, if you feel your emotions are
getting in the way of his cooperation, take a moment. Before you
speak up, try looking again at the other person's side. Verbalize
to him your understanding of his position. Simply hearing your
words reflecting his feeling will predispose him to open up to your
side.

In any negotiation circumstance, be diplomatic and tactful.
Insults and affronts will only serve to alienate the person you're
trying to win over.

THE SECRET OF SUCCESSFUL NEGOTIATIONS

There is only one way to get somebody to do something you want. You have to give her something she wants in return.

Life is a "quid pro quo" arrangement. The Romans knew this thousands of years ago: one thing in return for another.

Sure, you can force a person by pointing a gun at her head. You can make an employee do something by threatening to fire her. You can bellow and bluster and otherwise try to intimidate your associates into going your way. But the instant the threat is removed, the person will retaliate.

The only way to negotiate anything is to give one thing in return for another.

So, what can you give? Money is often an incentive. So is a new title or an extra perk. But these cannot always be given, nor are they always most needed.

What all human beings desire and need most is a feeling of being appreciated, a feeling of being important. This goes back to the first key: "I am a most valuable person." You can influence another person to your side by paying value to her. Let her know she counts. A person whose self-esteem is gratified will be far more receptive to meeting you halfway.

THE TRIANGLE PRINCIPLE

There are a few easily understood rules to put into practical use when negotiating.

The first involves that we call the Triangle Principle of Successful Negotiations. Visualize a triangle in your mind. You are at one point; your boss, client, associate, or whoever is at another point; and the raise, promotion, work load, or whatever is being negotiated is at the third point.

The second, and perhaps the most important, aspect of negotiation is that each part of the triangle is *equal*. All three sides must win. No one loses. Each person must feel that he's satisfied, that he's gotten something. If one side feels he's been taken, it's not a good deal. The law of cause and effect will ultimately boomerang back with a slew of problems. But if the negotiation results in an agreement where all sides feel comfortable, the future is clear sailing.

Negotiation begins when you listen, really listen, to what the other person is saying. Don't be thinking of what you're going to say as soon as the other stops. Try to empathize and understand what the other person wants and why. You must also have a clear understanding of what you really want and what compromise you can live with.

Be totally truthful with yourself. Unless each person in the negotiation process understands the complete picture, you won't succeed in coming to a good agreement.

SIX RULES FOR STRATEGIC NEGOTIATION

1. Stick to the subject. If you are negotiating for a new title, don't ask for a raise at the same time. If you are introducing new procedures, don't bring up overtime in the same session. Talking about too many subjects dilutes the main point under negotiation. It can also cause communication "overload," in which the other person cannot assimilate all that you're saying. He may end up rejecting the entire package.

2. If it's necessary to negotiate several points at one meeting, have the subjects clearly delineated in your mind. (Better still, write them out.) In a systematic fashion, go down the list, tackling each point one at a time, until it is either agreed upon to your mutual satisfaction or you both agree to table the point until the next meeting.

3. Never trample on the other person's ego. Sarcasm, insults, and intimidation have a negative boomerang effect. A negotiation must end as a double-win; if the other person feels he has lost face, the agreement will ultimately fall through.

4. Sidestep any attempt by the other person to belittle you. If the conversation heats up, stay calm. Diplomatically return the tone to the topic at hand. If necessary, call for a time out. Arrange to meet on another day. Remember, it is equally important for you to feel satisfied with the outcome.

5. Be prepared to give some concessions. Negotiating is a give-and-take game. Determine in advance what you can live with, or do without. List them in order of their importance to you. Knowing you have something to give will allow you more flexibility in negotiating for what you want to take.

6. Under no circumstances give away something that is absolutely essential to you. In any negotiating encounter, there is a bottom line that can't be negotiated. Be fully aware what your bottom line is. Don't be like the bride-to-be who believes in fidelity, but agrees not to ask her fiancé questions in order to get to the altar. She ends up a jealous neurotic, her husband feels trapped, and the marriage goes on the rocks. If something is sacred to you,

do not negotiate it. Walk away from the bargaining table rather than compromise your principles.

NEGOTIATION IN ACTION

1. Rather than hearing what you want to hear, listen for the facts of the matter. Remember, everything you think is only your opinion, based upon your impressions from limited sources. In any negotiation, remain open-minded.

2. Give solution-oriented feedback when problem solving. Don't dwell on what went wrong. Instead, focus on what to *do next.* Spend your collective energies on moving forward toward finding the answer.

3. See both the positive and negative sides of the issue, and pursue the positive side.

4. There is no such thing as winning an argument. There is only winning an agreement.

Keep in mind the negotiator's motto:

If You Win, I Win Too.

DAY

Pride

GIVEN the choice of whether we should be proud or humble, a large percentage of us would say, "Pride is a sin. It's better to be humble."

In an exercise of humility, we say, "I'm just a working man," "I'm just an average guy," or "I'm just getting by."

What's the consequence of all this humble pie? Mediocrity. By insisting you're just this or only that or that you'll never amount to much or that you'll never be rich or that you'll never be happy with your job, your self-talk is taking you down the gullet of nonaccomplishment. You are programming yourself for mediocrity.

This is not what is meant by being humble. Humility does not mean you should waste your life or belittle your God-given talents.

Humility requires only that no matter what you do, you always recognize there is room for improvement. Humility means that you remain aware that there is a force much greater than you. Humility comes when you realize that in spite of all your failings, God still loves you and is proud of what you have accomplished.

That's what pride is. Pride is trying to be the best you can be, because it's your *effort* that pleases God. Herein lies one of the secrets to success and happiness on the job—it's not chasing after the dollar, but having pride in one's work that brings lasting joy.

PRIDE IS POSITIVE SELF-ESTEEM

Pride is not: self-depreciation, self-doubt, self-consciousness.

Pride does not have to mean an overhigh opinion of oneself. It's not being conceited, haughty, or arrogant.

Pride is: self-worth, self-respect, self-confidence. Pride is personal dignity. Pride is the inner satisfaction of a job well-done.

Unhappy individuals have little pride. Their self-talk repeats, "I'd rather be someone else, doing something else, somewhere else."

On the other hand, people who find daily joy in their life and work feel a deep sense of self-worth. Their self-talk is: "I like myself. I really do like myself. Given my parents and my background, I'm glad I'm me. I'd rather be living right now than in any other time in history."

Individuals who radiate such self-confidence weren't necessarily born with these good feelings, but they have learned to like themselves through practice. And because they like themselves, they can share their joy with others.

I'M GLAD I'M ME

When you come down to the bottom line, *joy is accepting yourself as you are right now*—an imperfect, changing, growing, and worthwhile person. Realize that liking yourself and feeling that you're an OK individual in your own special way is not necessarily egotistical. Take pride in what you are accomplishing and, even more importantly, enjoy the unique person you are just in being alive right now. Understand the truth that although we as individuals are not born with equal physical and mental attributes, we are born with equal rights to feel the excitement and joy in believing that we deserve the very best in life. Most successful people believe in their own worth, even when they have nothing but a dream to hold on to. Perhaps more than any other quality, healthy pride in oneself is the door to high achievement and happiness.

P—is for Pleasure. To feel pride is to feel pleasure, whether it is the good feeling that comes from a job well-done or the simple pleasure of being alive and being you.

R—is for Respect. To feel respect for yourself as a decent, upright individual whose word is his honor is the core to healthy and happy self-pride.

I—is for Improvement. To keep in mind that no human being is perfect and that we must always work on improving ourselves. This is what keeps "pride" from bloating into "prideful."

D—is for Dignity. To have dignity is to have an inner feeling of worthiness. It's a deep self-respect that doesn't require the roar of the crowd.

E—is for Effort. To have pride in something, you have to put in some effort to get it. Nothing of value comes easily. Ultimately, there can be no pride in something you've not worked for. Pride is the pleasure felt at the achievement of your efforts.

PRIDE IN ACTION

1. Don't brag about all the worthwhile things you're doing. Don't even talk of them. Let your actions speak for you.

2. Pride and humility are two sides of one coin. Pride is necessary to do your best. Humility is necessary to know you can do even better. Consistently do your best and persistently try to do even better. That's the coin that will bring you much wealth.

3. Hold yourself in high esteem, but make sure you have every good reason to do so.

4. Take pride in everything you do. Your work is a direct reflection of you. Do your job well and feel proud of your efforts and accomplishments.

The core of healthy pride is knowing
that:

Pride Is the
Pleasure of Your Efforts.

DAY

25

Faith

HERE is a power that is open to all people, yet very few individuals use it consciously in their daily work life. With it comes the promise of realization of one's hopes and dreams. Without it, there is emptiness, fear, and a meaningless existence.

What is this power?

Faith.

Faith is an unquestioning belief. Faith is complete trust and confidence. Faith is positive, enriching life in the here and now. Faith can be found in all houses of spiritual belief and also in nature. Most importantly, faith is found in the hearts and souls of each of us. Faith is the key to unlock the door of success and happiness for every human being.

When we talk about faith—and belief and trust—we have to turn to the greatest book ever written. It holds the eternal wisdom of all ages: "According to your faith be it unto you." (Matthew 9:29.)

This simple statement cuts both ways, like a two-edged sword. Have faith, and all things are possible. Faith is the source of all human strength and courage. The man or woman who believes will be strong; those who have no convictions will flounder. But there is no such thing as the absence or lack of faith. There is only the replacement of faith with its opposite belief—doubt and despair.

BODY AND SOUL

Faith and science are merging based on studies carried out in the past decade about how the human brain functions. Although we have much to learn in understanding the mechanisms in the brain and central nervous system, we are aware of the inextricable relationship between psyche and soma—mind and body. There is a definite reaction that occurs in the body as a result of the thoughts of the mind. What the human soul harbors, the body manifests in some way.

When your thoughts are combined with faith, if you deeply *believe*, you will receive courage and strength to help you along the way. Your subconscious mind is prepared to carry out definite plans for achieving your goals.

All thoughts that are founded in faith begin immediately to transform themselves into their physical manifestations.

Faith actually has the power to affect the chemistry of the brain. When belief is combined with thought, neurotransmitters instantly pick up the interaction. The subconscious mind is then chemically geared to carry out the thoughts of the soul in the action of the body.

One of the greatest inspirationalists of our time, Dr. Norman Vincent Peale, puts it this way: "Religious faith may very well be considered a science, for it responds invariably to certain formulae. Perform the technique of faith according to the laws which have been proved workable in human experience and you will always get a result of power."

When we talk of prayer, we recognize that the uniting of faith and thought ignites a spiritual spark transmitted to God. God receives the prayer and then completes the circle of energy by helping and strengthening us in our daily endeavors. Faith gives us the courage to live and do.

Psychologists interpret this phenomenon as the self-fulfilling prophecy. Samuel I. Hayakawa refers to the self-fulfilling prophecy as a statement that is not necessarily true or false, but is capable of becoming true if it is believed. We have already learned the importance of self-talk and positive visualization. When it comes to brain activity, the mind can't distinguish between something that is real and something that is vividly imagined. That is why the concepts of faith and belief are so important to the joy of working.

Faith is a state of mind that can be created, repeated, and practiced. For many individuals, prayer is the most powerful form of self-talk.

DEAD-ENDS

Lack of faith leads to despair. Yet, so many individuals have lived so long without any sense of belief they have come to accept despair as normal. They sense there is something missing in their lives, that their lives lack glow and meaning, but figure that money or prestige or kicks will do the trick.

We live in a privileged society with an abundance of material goods and comforts. We have come to believe that pain is unacceptable, that stress can be cured in sixty seconds, that success is just a minute away.

We want to have love, happiness, and fulfillment, but have difficulty sticking it out when faced with challenges and setbacks. Without an overriding faith, despair seeps in.

What results is an escape from the type of commitment and

sacrifices that are necessary to building an intimate relationship with another human being or a fulfilling, satisfying lifetime career.

One escape route is through sexual promiscuity. So many sad, searching individuals try to find lasting happiness in bed, but come to a dead-end of unwanted pregnancy, venereal disease, or loneliness.

Another dead-end is through drug abuse. Drugs produce an unnatural high. When people use drugs, they don't have to make an effort to achieve instant pleasure—but they are robbed of the feeling of pride. Workers all over the country are using drugs—maybe it's pot for the construction worker, maybe it's cocaine for the stockbroker—trying to shortcut the lasting means to self-satisfaction and pride. Instead, they end up short-circuited victims of depression, dependency, and despair.

We must also include alcohol in this category. Too many Mondays are lost to hangovers. Too many afternoons are set adrift after liquid lunches.

People who are "doing drugs" are trying to escape from all the bad news in their lives.

It's time for some good news. The discovery of faith can pull a person up short—and turn his life around.

HAVE FAITH IN YOURSELF

One of the major reasons people turn to liquor, pills, and compulsive sexual behavior is the sad fact that they have so little faith in themselves. So they look for that faith in the bottle or between the sheets. Dead-end streets, all of it.

Faith in yourself begins with the understanding that God is always with you and within you. You needn't look outside for faith—you've already got it. All you have to do is recognize it.

God created you, therefore you are inherently worthy. "The Kingdom of God is within you." (Luke 17:21.) Now, that's power. Begin to firmly believe in the constant flow of God's power through you. Fill your mind with thoughts of faith and confidence. Think, "God has confidence in me," and you'll soar through whatever you endeavor.

God is with you; God is helping you; God is guiding you. This is one of the foundations of *all* spiritual teaching. It's the most powerful idea to positively affect the lives of ordinary men and women. Practice believing this thought. Think it frequently throughout your workday. Visualize it, feel it. The faith you develop in yourself will astonish you.

THE CENTER OF JOY AND SUCCESS

Some people try to put a straitjacket on God. He belongs only in church, or only with the pious, or only on the Sabbath. Worse is the erroneous belief that God somehow rewards certain individuals with wealth. If only you pray hard enough, the Lord will "buy" you what you want.

There is a disturbing philosophical movement today that associates happiness and contentment with materialistic power and gain. Ultimately, there can be no joy in working when the mind is obsessed with money, politics, and the bottom line.

"No man is an island." To exist, to work just for yourself is meaningless. You can achieve most when you feel related to some greater purpose in life, something greater than yourself. Whether you are a successful homemaker or computer programmer or businessman, you must somehow sense that you are in tune with God's purposes to fully enjoy your work and the fruits of your labor.

Material rewards must be placed in perspective. The purpose of work is not to be a slave to your house, your car, your possessions. That's not the purpose we are here to fulfill on earth. Each of us has the potential to be the best we can be, and there is pure personal pleasure in achieving the difficult. Believe in yourself, your work, your fellow workers, and the ultimate attainment of a more complete happiness.

Each of us has to find our own relationship with our Maker and try to live up to all God wants us to be.

FAITH IN ACTION

1. If you become depressed, if your burdens become too heavy, try this: "Let go and let God." Let go of your troubles and let God help you. Talk to God. Tell Him what's troubling you. Do this with an open heart; you'll feel His strength flow through you.

2. Pray. Prayer is the most powerful form of self-talk. It can actually affect the brain's chemistry, preparing your soul with strength and courage to carry you toward your dreams and goals.

3. Get high on doing good. No one yet in the history of mankind has found lasting satisfaction in liquor or chemicals. Real pleasure is had in good work, generous deeds, grateful thoughts.

4. Take one day a week to renew your faith and replenish your spirit. Get into the habit of attending religious services, listening, learning, sharing.

Joy of working means having faith in God
and therefore faith in yourself because you
are God's creation:

Believe
And You Can.

DAY

26

Purpose

To enjoy work, one must know that one is somehow moving forward to a goal. The feeling of working aimlessly, in circles, in a vacuum, is anathema to productivity. You can't do a job well with blinders on.

Not all jobs are good at providing workers with a sense of direction; some bosses are under the mistaken impression that they can achieve high productivity when employees are in the dark. And let's face it, some jobs are a dead-end. But none of that matters.

What is important is that *you* have purpose, that you feel your energies and time are taking you *somewhere*.

Think of the actress working as a waitress. She doesn't mind the tedium, because she knows where she is going. Or the medical intern doing "scut-work" at low pay who keeps his mind on the goal: to learn his specialty. The only true happiness comes from working hard for a purpose.

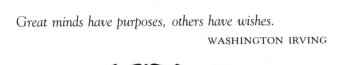

Great minds have purposes, others have wishes.

WASHINGTON IRVING

The real difference between people is purpose. A strong sense of purpose can accomplish almost anything. Purpose not only makes the difference between joy and misery, but it is also the most important key to life itself.

PRISONERS OF WORK

Without a sense of purpose, work becomes a prison. A man's (or a woman's) spirit an be eroded until he is reduced to an automaton, a robot, just a cog in the machine.

Without purpose, a man labors but he never achieves; he is constantly busy but he never gets anything done; he feels pressure but never produces; he has plenty of problems but no solutions; he knows a lot of people but knows nothing of people; he has a number of irons in the fire, but they're all on the back burner; he wants to get there fast but keeps running in circles.

Without purpose, work and life become meaningless exercises in futility.

Purpose is the engine that powers our lives. For some individuals, their purpose for working is to pay the rent. For others, it is simply to get through the day. For still others, it is to beat out the other guy, amass power, be number one.

Joyful workers, on the other hand, find a different purpose for working: to seek personal growth, to make a contribution, to find creative expression, to take part in discovery and challenge, and to develop sharing, cooperative relationships with others. These are the common goals that make uncommon people.

COMING FULL CIRCLE

The real winners in the game of life have developed a clear sense of purpose. They look beyond themselves for meaning in life. They integrate all the facets of their lives into a whole. To find joy of working, it is vital to gain perspective on ourselves in life and look at the big picture, the full circle of life.

One of the finest definitions of complete happiness was given by an anonymous Greek:

Happiness is the exercise of one's vital abilities along lines of excellence in a life that affords them scope.

Fulfillment is defined as the progressive realization of goals that are worthy of the individual. It seems that happiness and success come together when you are "doing your thing," when you recognize you are doing what suits you best, when your activities earn you the respect of other people, when your work benefits other people as well as yourself.

Consider the words of Albert Einstein:

Strange is our situation here upon earth. Each of us comes for a short visit, not knowing why, yet sometimes seeming to divine a purpose.

From the standpoint of daily life, however, there is one thing we do know: that man is here for the sake of other men—above all for those upon whose smile and well-being our own happiness depends, and also for the countless unknown souls with whose fate we are connected by a bond of sympathy. Many times a day I realize how much my own outer and inner life is built upon the labors of my fellow men, both living and dead, and how earnestly I must exert myself in order to give in return as much as I have received.

One of the great paradoxes of life is that happiness cannot be directly achieved. True happiness is a *by-product* of a life full of purpose. Joy comes in seeking other things, in a life aimed at something outside oneself, in the full experience of all facets of life, and in the healthy outgoing, outgiving of all human powers, guided by some supreme purpose that gives our life unity and direction.

LOOK FOR PURPOSE
BEYOND YOURSELF

The joy of working comes in having a worthy destination and looking beyond yourself for meaning in life. One of the most prominent qualities displayed by people with purpose is the quality of earning the love and respect of other human beings.

Earlier in this book, we said that success does not mean standing victoriously over a conquered enemy. You are successful when you can extend a strong hand to someone who is reaching, or searching, or just trying to hang on. There is divine purpose in bringing out the best in one another.

Purposeless people live narrow lives. Their self-talk is "I'm only concerned about me, today."

The real leaders in life look for purpose beyond themselves. They say, "I live every moment, enjoying as much, relating as much, doing as much, and giving as much as I possibly can."

There is meaning in life beyond the job, beyond making the proverbial buck. Individuals who focus so narrowly on these goals frequently find themselves in a midlife crisis. They may have achieved the vice-presidency and have money to spend, but for what . . . ? It's a common cry of middle-aged careerists: "I worked so hard for so long, for what?"

The joy of working means knowing *why* you're working. It means working hard, working long hours, but for a *purpose*—the purpose of success, wealth, and, most important, *happiness.*

Take time along the way to learn the meaning of your life, your purpose here on earth.

People who have the full joy of working get together with loved ones, their friends and neighbors. They love their careers but are not married to them. They care about performance, productivity, and profit, but also effectiveness, fairness, and honesty.

Ultimately, the joy of purpose goes beyond human relationships. It applies very definitely to an individual's relationship with nature and its Creator. Perhaps more important than any other key that makes up the joy of working system is the ability to tap that tremendous abundance beyond ourselves, the spiritual dimension that is our own creation.

PURPOSE IN ACTION

1. Ask yourself the question: What is my purpose to fulfill with my family, my company, my profession, my community, my nation, my world, and my Creator?

2. What are your lifetime goals? What do you stand for? What are you working toward? What do you want your children to tell their children about you?

3. Make time once a week to do some introspection and soul-searching. A person's true greatness lies in the consciousness of an honest purpose in life.

Winners in life know there is much more to working than earning a living. They know:

Happiness Comes From Having a Purpose.

DAY

27

Wealth

IF you are developing a lifestyle that is pleasing and inspiring, and if your efforts are setting a healthy example for those who look to you for guidance and encouragement, you are indeed a wealthy person.

Wealth is a condition of being. Having much money is only one aspect of wealth. The idea of wealth actually depends on the value you place on all the bountiful riches life has to offer.

There are people who have six-figure incomes and Swiss bank accounts but are impoverished in spirit and happiness. There are people who have to struggle each month to pay the bills and put food on the table, but who are filled with the joy of working, the joy of their family, the joy of living.

Real poverty stems from the losing habits of self-criticism, chain-smoking, excessive drinking, overeating, procrastination, laziness, anxiety, depression, sloppiness, gluttony, dishonesty, cynicism, cruelty, and insensitivity.

More important than monetary riches, more important even than physical health, is a person's spirit. It is through the spirit that all wealth comes, and that includes the endurance to overcome ill health and survive times of financial hardship. The individual with a strong character will always make friends and draw support. It's a sure way to success, wealth, and happiness.

———————◆━●●━◆———————

A man's true wealth is the good he does in this world.

MUHAMMAD

———————◆━●●━◆———————

Remember, wealth is not only what you *have,* but also what you *are.*

IS WEALTH WRONG?

Many of us are prevented from using our talents because we live under the mistaken belief that it is wrong to be rich. We have the notion that it is noble to be poor. That poverty leads to spiritual purity. We rationalize from the Scriptures, "Money is the root of all evil," not realizing we're misquoting God's wisdom that "the *love* of *money* is the root of all evil." Indeed, much of the evil in the world today derives from people who have made money their god. When money, power, and personal gain are the chief aims in life, moral and economic crises follow, not only for the individual, but for the entire society.

Is it then inherently evil to acquire wealth? No. If money is the result of our efforts and labor, if the by-products of our work benefit others, and if our wealth is used to give comfort and security to those we love, then money is indeed a *good* to be acquired.

Listen to what Norman Vincent Peale has to say about wealth: "The man who lives for himself is a failure. Even if he gains much wealth, position, or power, he is still a failure. The man who lives for others has achieved true success. A rich man who consecrates his wealth and his position to the good of humanity is a success. A poor man who gives of his service and his sympathy to others has achieved true success, even though material prosperity or outward honors never come to him."

———————◆—●:●—◆———————

We have no more right to consume happiness without producing it, than to consume wealth without producing it.

GEORGE BERNARD SHAW

———————◆—●:●—◆———————

Money itself is a neutral element. A great deal of it is not necessarily a blessing, the lack of it not necessarily a curse. Certainly, it is easier to have a wholesome abundance than not. It is better for mankind to have enough for daily needs plus a little extra for comfort, for culture, for hospitality, for charity.

Extreme poverty and extreme wealth often have equally negative effects on our human nature and our society. The destitute have no money for their needs, much less creature comforts. They can't give to others, for they are charity cases themselves. The very rich are sometimes no better. Some purposefully neglect the comforts of home and family. Think of the recluse multi-millionaire Howard Hughes—he denied himself even food and proper medical care. There are wealthy individuals who never give a dime for church or charity. Some monied folks are begrudging to their friends and disdainful of others less fortunate than themselves.

Wealth is only a source of happiness when it is used to do good for others. To quote the indomitable Dolly Levi, the wise matchmaker in the musical *Hello, Dolly!*:

———————◆—●:●—◆———————

Money is like manure. It doesn't do anybody any good until you spread it around.

———————◆—●:●—◆———————

PRACTICAL THINKING
ABOUT MONEY

Only three out of every one hundred Americans reach age sixty-five with any degree of financial security. Ninety-seven out of one hundred Americans who are sixty-five and over must depend on their monthly Social Security checks to survive. These are cold facts supplied by the U.S. Department of Labor. Is this because the American dream is a myth? Is it because of runaway inflation or stagflation or recession? Is it because of the OPEC cartel or the military budget or the billion-dollar deficit? World economic conditions certainly have an effect on our financial situations. It is more difficult to survive and thrive during economic periods when the value of the dollar is eroded. There are, however, personal considerations that are equally as relevant as the environmental circumstances.

Would it surprise you to learn that only five of every one hundred Americans, who are in the higher-income professions such as law and medicine, reach age sixty-five without having to depend on Social Security?

Regardless of their level of income during their most productive years, astoundingly few individuals achieve any degree of financial security. Most people live their lives under the delusion that they are immortal. They squander their money, their time, and their minds with activities that are "tension relieving." They buy on impulse and live on credit. If you've ever wondered why paydays are on Thursdays and Fridays, it's because if they were on Mondays or Tuesdays, most people couldn't stretch their paychecks to last through the following weekend.

The vast majority of Americans hope that the winds of fate will blow them into some rich and mysterious port of call. They look forward to when they can retire "someday" and live on a fantasy island "somewhere." When asked how they will accomplish this, they respond, "Somehow."

People tend to spend more time planning a Christmas party or a vacation than they do their financial futures. By failing to plan, they actually are planning to fail.

There is an old saying: "If we command our wealth, we shall be rich and free; if our wealth commands us, we are poor indeed."

A hard look at your finances will be necessary to gain control of your capital. Sit down and ask yourself these questions about yourself and your work.

1. What are your spending habits? Can you account for your outflow of money?

2. What are your saving habits? Do you put away at least ten percent of each paycheck into a savings or investment account?

3. What is your major financial goal for next year? Are you saving for a new car, a vacation, a business investment? How much are you putting away each month toward this goal?

4. What is your current professional level and annual income? What will it be in five years?

5. What will be your assets, in dollars, ten years from now? Twenty years from now?

When it comes to planning your future and your wealth, these are some of the most important questions you must consider.

Money certainly cannot buy happiness. But the wise use of it can lead to wealth and joy.

WEALTH IN ACTION

1. Develop a healthy respect for your finances. Money should not be loved, hoarded, or wasted. Instead, use your earnings as an asset toward achieving your goals.

2. Continue your education regardless of your age. Studies indicate that older adults do ten percent better in college classes than their younger student associates. Put your money where your mind is.

3. Don't depend upon the government for your long-range financial security. Pay yourself each month by putting a sum of money into a savings account for your future. You are your best social security.

4. Count your wealth in the common pleasures—home, health, children. Think more about the worth of individuals and less about their wealth.

5. Wealth is a state of mind. You can acquire a wealthy state of mind by thinking rich thoughts.

Wealth is counted not only in dollars and cents, but also in decency and sense. The joy of money comes in knowing:

Wealth Is Not Only What You Have, But Also What You Are.

DAY

28

Power

WE are but sleepwalking until we awaken the power of our minds. The greatest power of all is not in ruling others or commanding great wealth, but in commanding the brain's thinking process. That's where all power begins. The wonderful thing is that this power is available to each one of us—if only we try.

The great writer Ralph Waldo Emerson observed, "We do not yet trust the unknown powers of thought." No matter who he is or what job he holds, it is the man who *uses his brain* who will gain the most power.

How can you harness your brainpower? Let's look at what "power" is.

P—Power is purpose. Ideas, dreams, goals, any product of the mind's eye harnessed to a purpose will produce a storehouse of power.

O—Power is open-mindedness. It is having a mind open to new ideas. It is thinking unfettered by preconceived notions.

W—Power is wisdom. It means strength, tempered by good judgment, combined with learning and knowledge.

E—Power is energy. It is the engine of work, the force of human expression, the capacity for action.

R—Power is responsibility. The greater the power, the greater the responsibility. Power without responsibility leads to corruption and evil. Power united to responsibility is the source of good works and the increased well-being of all.

In short, the definition of power is not force or manipulation or domination over others. Power is the ability, the vigor, the strength to influence others and to control one's own destiny.

THE POWER PRINCIPLE

Power is often considered to be in the sole domain of a few people: the foreman, the boss, the executive vice-president, the C.E.O. Unfortunately, many employees feel rather powerless in their jobs.

The truth is, each one of us possesses power. God gave us this power when he gave us the ability to choose. Power means having the ability to choose among the many possibilities open to us and the freedom to act upon them in order to shape the direction of our lives.

Most powerful is he who has himself in his own power.

SENECA

People who are aware that they have the power to take control of their lives are generally much happier on the job. They feel they have the power within them to respond appropriately to whatever situation they encounter in their workday. Power is not to be confused with "throwing your weight around." Power is being able to adapt, to negotiate, to plan, to take responsibility, and, most importantly, to feel in control of your behavior.

KNOWLEDGE IS POWER

This statement should be displayed in every office, in every factory, in every service center in America. *Knowledge is power.* We've all heard the statement and we recognize its truth.

So, why don't more people believe it and put it into practice? Why do so few people continue their education after they've graduated from high school or college? Why do only five percent of Americans buy and read nonfiction books?

One reason is a lack of self-esteem. So many people don't believe they are worth the time and effort it takes to learn about new subjects or study other subjects in greater depth: "I was never good in school," "I'm not very academically minded," "I don't think books have anything to do with the real world."

This brings us to the second reason. Many people don't believe that information found in books is valuable in the business world. How wrong they are! As the computer and word processor become the new tools of productivity, the individuals who know how to control these new technologies will be the people with power. Those who thought that education ends with the diploma will be more likely to end up in low-paying, low-satisfaction jobs. Our society has passed from the Industrial Age into the Information Age. Knowledge and information are the keys to opportunity and advancement.

But the third reason why most people avoid learning is that

they are too lazy. These are individuals who prefer to do the least possible, just enough to get by. Reading, learning, studying smacks too much of hard work. It's just easier to put your brain on hold while you go through the motions of the workday. Actually, if people spent half as much time reading as they waste staring at the tube, they could immeasurably increase their learning and earning power.

Unhappy workers sense that the rest of the world has one leg up on them, that other people control the job environment.

Joyful workers are aware that they have some degree of control over their destinies. That's because they constantly practice the power of knowledge.

Whether you are a salesman, in business, a teacher, a homemaker, a laborer, or an executive, education will always serve you better than ignorance.

Knowledge stems from keeping an open mind and from the hard work of self-improvement. As someone once said, "There is no knowledge that is not power."

We take this to mean *applied knowledge.* Intellectualism is the empty exercise of ego-starved individuals. But *knowledge tied to a purpose*—to make a better living, provide better service, create an improved life for our family and society—that is the power that can be harnessed to accomplish a hundred things.

THERE'S POWER IN THEM THAR WORDS

In George Orwell's classic work aimed against totalitarianism, *Nineteen Eighty-Four,* he describes the language of "newspeak." Big Brother's plan was to systematically reduce the number of words people could use. The fewer the words, the fewer the ideas, the less thinking, the less power to the people.

Frighteningly enough, Orwell's vision is coming true in this country, but not through government's dictates. Linguistic experts estimate that the average citizen's vocabulary level is decreasing about one percent a year. Only 400 words make up over eighty percent of our daily conversations, but there are over 450,000 in the English language. (And remember, "I," "me," "my," and "mine" are the most commonly used words of all.)

The ability, or inability, to express our thoughts in words is one of the most important distinctions that separates successful workers from the rest of the population. No matter what the arena of employment, it is those individuals with a large vocabulary who manage to do best in accomplishing their goals. This is a fact based on research by management and human-resource experts. The power of words is immense. Well-chosen, carefully considered words can close the sale, negotiate a raise, enhance worker relationships. Knowledge is power, and a broad knowledge of language is the key that unlocks the door.

THE PROBLEM OF POWER

Handling power—yours or the boss's—can be one of the most significant sore points in working relationships.

Some people tend to let power go to their heads. They become authoritarian, dogmatic, and arrogant. They think they can get away with insulting or demeaning behavior toward others. They begin to believe they are invincible, infallible. The British nobleman Lord Acton wrote that "Power tends to corrupt and absolute power corrupts absolutely." Men intoxicated with power wreak emotional and social havoc in the lives of people who must work under them—and economic havoc for their company and the marketplace. Needless to say, absolute power in world leaders disintegrates into dictatorships and war.

There are but two powers in the world, the sword and the mind. In the long run, the sword is always beaten by the mind.

NAPOLEON

We realize that power has a negative connotation. Yet power, like money, is a neutral substance. It can be used for evil or for good. Power in the right hands can be used to help others, to create new jobs, to establish business enterprises.

People should be proud of their abilities to achieve their goals. They should use their personal power to learn, to grow, and to excel. This is power used positively.

Problems arise when power is used negatively against others, or when it enlarges the ego to the point where the individual begins to think he or she is special or destined to control others. The power monger's motto is, "Rules are for others to follow, for me to break."

The joy of power comes in knowing that "no matter how successful or wealthy I become, my values and relationships will remain constant."

It is the individual who uses his powers in the right way who will be better able to find satisfaction in any occupation, whether it is tightening the bolts on a steering column or steering a corporation into the future.

The very essence of power lies in the ability to create a win-win situation. The person who can accomplish that will possess most of the power he'll ever need to accomplish his goals.

Remember also that power and responsibility go hand in hand. Each one of us is accountable for his or her use of power. Used responsibly, power is a force for good.

POWER IN ACTION

1. The fundamental principle of power is the knowledge that you control your own emotions and responses to a given situation. Always keep in mind that it's not so much what happens in life; it's how you take it and what you make of it.

2. There is power in language. If you cannot understand certain words being said or written, or if you cannot express your feelings accurately and clearly, you will feel powerless with others. Make the dictionary your best-seller book. Learn a new word every day. Make it a point to look up any unfamiliar word you come across. Sit down and actually read a page a day in your dictionary. Next to the Bible, the dictionary is the best "power" book on the market.

3. Knowledge is power. Learn all you can about your company and the business your company is in. Invest in your knowledge. Take a course or read a book about your industry. Enroll in an extension course at your local college or university. Develop some aspect of your professional career.

Real power is not brute force:

Brainpower Is
The Most Potent Power of
All.

DAY

29

Wisdom

W
ISDOM is:

- having good judgment.
- being open and informed.
- acting sharp in practical affairs.
- learning from the experiences of others.
- the right use of knowledge.

No one is born with wisdom. Children, for example, are rarely wise—unless we take the word to mean precocious, which can have the subtle connotation of self-centered manipulation. No, wisdom is a quality that develops slowly over the years. Wisdom can't be inherited, but it can be learned, nurtured, and practiced. As the Greek philosopher and mathematician Pythagoras wrote twenty-six centuries ago, "Wisdom thoroughly learned will never be forgotten."

So, what is wisdom in practical terms? Wisdom can be summed up as *adapting to new information and situations while incorporating past experiences.*

Wisdom is not simply the storing of vast quantities of information. Trivia experts, for example, know astoundingly numerous things, but that has nothing to do with wisdom. Scholars, too, may have studied long years in their field of expertise, but intellectual giants are often very foolish when it comes to practical affairs.

Wisdom is the practical ability to take facts, feelings, and instincts and form a rational judgment founded on experience and maturity.

The most successful people in the work world are those who have found ways to combine past experiences with present circumstances to create a bountiful future.

That is wisdom in action.

THE BIG PICTURE

A major component of wisdom is perspective. Put another way, this means seeing the "big picture." The worker who finds satisfaction in his or her labors understands the big picture and sees how he or she is a part of it.

During World War II, parachutes were being constructed by the thousands. From the worker's point of view, the job was tedious. It involved crouching over a sewing machine eight to ten hours a day, stitching endless lengths of colorless fabric. The result was a formless heap of cloth. But every morning, the workers were told that each stitch was part of a lifesaving operation. As they sewed, they were asked to think that this might be the parachute worn by their husband, their brother, their son.

Although the work was hard and the hours long, the women and men on the home front understood their contribution to the larger picture.

The same should apply to every occupation, in every time. The file clerk who sees every account as representing a human being with aspirations and dreams. The auto-assembly worker who knows each car is taking a family safely on their journeys. The bank teller who understands each customer is working and saving, as she is, toward personal and professional goals.

Wisdom comes from the perspective of seeing how you fit in with the grander designs of this world and the universe.

THE WISDOM OF COUNTING YOUR BLESSINGS

It's been said that with some hard work and determination, it's relatively easy to get what you want. The hard part is enjoying yourself once you have it.

We know executives with corner offices overlooking a magnificent city skyline who never look out the window.

We know successful businessmen who own fabulous houses in the country but only come home to eat and sleep.

We know well-to-do employees who buy on credit and have a great car and new furniture, but are never satisfied because "the Joneses" just got something better.

Do you know people like these? Of course you do. The world is full of people who count their troubles every night before going to bed and repeat the litany on their way to work.

The truly wise individual counts his blessings, starting with the greatest blessing of all—being alive and healthy enough to work. Be glad you have a job or that you are training for one or that you have legs to carry you as you look for one. Be glad for your weekly paycheck, which goes toward feeding your family and into savings for future pleasures. Be thankful for the people who surround you at work, for friendships are among the best blessings of life.

You can probably go on to list other blessings about your particular circumstance—the people you've hired, your supervisor who is becoming your mentor, the challenge of your job, the customers who make your work possible, the contribution you are making toward a better world.

The joy of working is seeing the brighter side to even difficult circumstances. Tom A., for example, is radio dispatcher for his county's emergency services. Unfortunately, it's swing-shift work that changes every week—eight to four, or four to midnight, or midnight to eight A.M. His body clock never has a chance to stabilize. A regular lifestyle is virtually impossible to keep. Does Tom count his troubles? Just the opposite. He is thankful that his unusual schedule allows him entire weeks when he can be home during the day with his infant son. His working wife also appreciates the flexibility. Since one of them is almost always home, they need not spend money on a baby-sitter or day-care and instead can save for their child's education.

Two hundred years ago, the eminent English writer Dr. Samuel Johnson said, "The habit of looking on the best side of every event is worth more than a thousand pounds a year."

The joy of working comes from the wisdom of *counting your blessings, never your troubles.* True wisdom lies in recognizing, appreciating, and being thankful for all the precious moments in our daily working lives.

THE FULL LIFE

At the end of his working career, the wise man (or woman) looks back and thinks, "I have enjoyed every day of the journey."

The unhappy worker is bitter: "I worked myself to the bone, and now I'm too old to enjoy the fruits of my labors."

DAY 29

The joy of working means working hard, but also enjoying life along the way.

Wisdom is gained by being open to and enjoying all the facets of life. Check yourself with this questionnaire.

	(Yes)	(No)	(Sometimes)
1. Do you spend enough quality time with your family, giving, sharing, and loving?	( )	( )	( )
2) Are you involved with your community, neighbors, friends?	( )	( )	( )
3) Do you allow for some private time every day to recoup and regenerate?	( )	( )	( )
4) Are you taking care of your physical health through proper nutrition and exercise?	( )	( )	( )
5) Do you take pleasure in the work that you do to earn a living?	( )	( )	( )
6) Are you consistently developing your skills and knowledge related to your profession?	( )	( )	( )
7) Do you have a sound and workable budget for spending and saving?	( )	( )	( )
8) Do you regularly attend church, synagogue, or religious services?	( )	( )	( )
9) Do you daily appreciate the blessings of nature, the seasons, fields and woods, the sun at noon, and the midnight stars?	( )	( )	( )
10) Do you feel at ease in life and with your position in it?	( )	( )	( )

Take a look at your responses. We can't pretend that a "yes" guarantees you wisdom, but we think you'll see that work, play, and prayer must join together to create a full life.

We'd like to end this day with this thought:

———————◆—◗●◖—◆———————

Live your life each day as you would climb a mountain. An occasional glance toward the summit keeps the goal in mind, but many beautiful scenes are to be observed from each new vantage point. Climb slowly, steadily, enjoying each passing moment; and the view from the summit will serve as a fitting climax for the journey.

HAROLD V. MELCHERT

———————◆—◗●◖—◆———————

WISDOM IN ACTION

1. Take time out of every working day to observe the wonder and beauty of nature. During coffee breaks, find a window or doorway and look out. If you have an hour for lunch, eat at your desk and then take a half-hour or forty-five-minute walk outside.

2. Look at the "big picture." No matter how important or how insignificant you think your work is, it is all part of the greater design of life. No task is an end unto itself. Develop a philosophy that helps you put you and your labors in perspective.

3. Count your blessings daily. In times of trouble especially, count your blessings. As you recognize your bounties, you'll find added strength to press forward.

4. Remember that a full life incorporates your social life, your spiritual life, your physical health, the love of your family, the development of sound financial planning, and professional satisfaction.

Joy wells up when you know you lead a good
life, work hard, and learn:

Wisdom
Is the Right Use of
Knowledge.

DAY

30

Success

DAY 30

IT'S been said that the greatest failure of our time is equating success solely with material possessions.

When we think of success, we tend to think of two questions:

1. Do other people think I'm a success?
2. Do I think I'm a success?

Success, in order to be meaningful, is a very personal thing. Too often we narrow our ideas about success to fit the popular molds. We spend a great deal of effort and money trying to display how successful we are—or wish we were—with big cars, new houses, fur coats, country club memberships, exclusive vacations. What is the meaning behind all this posturing? Why are we trying so hard to prove something to someone else? Or are we trying to prove something to ourselves? A feeling of inner success is much harder to acquire. It requires questioning about what we really want out of life.

George Sand, the nineteenth-century novelist, defined five necessary ingredients for enjoying success.

1. Simple tastes.

2. A certain degree of courage.

3. Self-denial to a point.

4. Love of work.

5. A clear conscience.

The fifth ingredient, a clear conscience, is absolutely essential to enjoying success. There was a wealthy, successful, and happy Manhattan real estate broker who confided, "I could have made a lot more money in my life, but I preferred to sleep well at night."

The ideal is to achieve outward as well as inner success. But all success must be built from the inside out.

Sleeping well after a good day at earnest work is one of the joys of life. People who can't find peace with themselves in their own beds often end up on psychiatrists' couches. Psychiatrists grow rich from individuals who cannot enjoy what they've earned. There are people who seem to have everything but go from shrink to guru to cult hero trying to discover some joy in their life. Some have all the outer trappings of success but feel empty inside.

DO YOU DESERVE SUCCESS?

Deep inside, you may think you're unworthy. "I've fouled up a lot in my life," you say. "My father said I'd never amount to much." "My mother always criticized me." "My wife says I don't earn enough." "So how can I be worthy of success?"

You probably look at others and see they are smarter or younger or older or harder working or more clever or better looking. You probably think they deserve more success than you do.

Success is not a pie, with only so many slices to go around. The success of others has nothing to do with your success.

Nor is your success measured by what others say or what others accomplish. We all have the tendency to compare ourselves with others. But the happy people in this life know it's not against others that we compete.

The late Henry Fonda once said that a thoroughbred horse never looks at the other racehorses. It just concentrates on running the fastest race it can.

On our track to success, we have to fight the tendency to look at others and see how far they've come. The only thing that counts is how we use the potential we possess, that we run our race to the best of our abilities.

Success is not handed to anyone on a silver platter. No one is entitled to happiness, a good job, lots of money. Success must be earned. The only way to earn it is to utilize whatever combination of talent, skill, and intelligence you possess to the fullest extent possible.

Do you deserve success? Absolutely. You owe it to yourself.

SUCCESS AND SATISFACTION

There is a direct relationship between joy and effort. The joy of success is in ratio to the amount of effort expended to achieve it.

The man who will use his skill and constructive imagination to see how much he can give for a dollar, instead of how little he can give for a dollar, is bound to succeed.

HENRY FORD

Personal satisfaction is the most important ingredient of success. It's a very individual definition—for one man it might be closing a sale, for another it's painting a picture. But neither man is successful if he finds no satisfaction in closing a sale or painting a picture.

Success must be enjoyed. Success is the ultimate pinnacle of the joy of working.

But success is not a constant. Napoleon once said, "The most dangerous moment comes with victory."

It's about this time, when outer success seems at hand, that we give up finding true success. Overconfidence sets in; we feel irritable when new problems arise. We believe success, once earned, should be permanent.

The trouble is most of us have not disentangled outer, public success with personal, inner success. Only the latter can lead to true happiness.

Success must be constantly renewed.

So what is success really all about? What are the secrets to lasting success that bring self-satisfaction and joy? We know what the outer trappings of success are. What are the hallmarks of inner success?

Success brings us joy when it is coupled with:

- perspective—understanding and accepting your part in the world and God's universe.
- self-esteem—We started this book with self-esteem, and it is a fine way to end a book on the joy of working.
- self-awareness—seeing yourself through others' eyes and liking what you see.
- wisdom—taking time to learn from the past, plan for the future, and enjoy the present as fully as possible.
- faith—a strong belief in a force greater than yourself. Success will never spoil an individual who believes in the grace of God.

- family—Having love and giving love are the greatest successes a person can count.

- double-win attitude—"If I help you win, then I win too." A truly successful individual has made his own fortune while helping to build the fortunes of others.

- nature—daily appreciating the wonders and the beauty of the world we live in.

- health—What good is power, money, and success if you don't have your health to enjoy it? A truly successful individual respects his or her body as a valuable treasure created by God.

- joy—feeling alive every moment, enjoying, sharing, working, and giving as much as possible to this glorious time we have here on earth.

INFINITE SUCCESS

You have been put here on earth to succeed. You don't have to apologize to anyone for being a success or for trying to succeed, since you have a responsibility, a noble obligation, to use your abilities to the fullest.

Wealth, honestly earned and well spent, is inherently good. Only the love of money leads to evil and unhappiness.

You don't have to suffer on earth in exchange for eternal happiness in heaven. If anything, our time on earth should be used to prepare ourselves for boundless joy to come, much as a parent's heart grows with love for each new child. Let your soul rejoice at the thrill and exaltation of life.

By granting you life, God gave you permission to succeed, to enjoy your life and your work.

To do this, you must control your own life. You were not created to be led by others. Prefer excellence to mediocrity. Accept total responsibility for yourself. Don't prevent your own success.

You deserve success, for all success requires is that you are here and use your talents to the fullest. Bring your talents to the world. Don't wait for the world to come to you. Act now, no matter how much better tomorrow may seem, no matter how imperfect the results you obtain might be.

Make constructive use of the abilities that you are blessed with. Take with you all the love and energy and talent you have and share it. Share it with all whom you meet, for you are infinite. Your potential extends beyond your wildest imagination. The only limitations you will ever face will be those you place upon yourself.

SUCCESS IN ACTION

1. Appreciate each moment of your working day. If the work gets boring, go right to the basics. Appreciate your hands or legs or brain, which function so efficiently. Use your powers of visualization to see yourself succeeding in your goals.

2. Take action. Success never falls into someone's lap. Inner and outer success is always the result of self-control, responsibility, preparation, and forward motion.

3. Motivate yourself. Practice positive thinking. Forget past failures. Focus on the rewards of success.

You understand now:

Enjoying Your Work Is The Secret to Success.

DAY

Joy

DAY 31

The object of living is work, experience, happiness. There is joy in work. All that money can do is buy us someone else's work in exchange for our own. There is no happiness except in the realization that we have accomplished something.

HENRY FORD

J OY is the forerunner and the consequence of success, wealth, and happiness. Joy starts within. It's a glad confirmation of your self-worth reflected by your work and accomplishments. Joy of working means keeping an inner smile in all that you do—and watching yourself prosper. Joy lights your face with the glow of success. It attracts others to you. You radiate confidence, and everyone wants to be associated with confidence and competence. Joy of working is the lubricant of all business and productivity. Yes, keep a smile in your heart—it's the spark that lights the world with success, wealth, and happiness.

What is joy? Joy is:

JOY

J—A Job Well-Done

O—Optimism

Y—You.

There is no more satisfying feeling than a *job well-done*. Doing your best never depletes you, but instead fills you with self-esteem and inner peace. The pleasures of life—an evening at home, a weekend of fishing, a saved-for vacation—are best enjoyed when they are your self-rewards for a job well-done.

Optimism and joy go hand in hand. Joy is the indelible, ardent knowledge that your life and work are ultimately for the good. Optimism is expecting the best from yourself and from others. It's the sure confidence that whatever curves are thrown your way, you will make the best out of any situation.

Ultimately, *joy is you*. You are the source of pleasure and satisfaction in your work. Joy cannot be found outside yourself, nor should it be confused with momentary ecstasy or "happy hour" escapism. TGIF parties are fun and bolster working friendships, but don't be like the man who harps, "My only delight is Friday night." Make every day a cause for joy: "Thank goodness it's today." Deep-down joy is a lasting feeling that colors all our experiences—uphill and down—and gives our work meaning and purpose.

Now that you understand the joy of working system, now that you're energized, motivated, and inspired to be all that you can be, share this book and spread the joy by buying your friends a copy. This book is yours to keep, to hold as a reference, to value as your guide to a satisfying, fulfilling career.

Read this book over again in the days and months to come. See how far you've progressed, understand where you still need improvement, review those passages that speak to your current work situation most directly. Underscore sections or paper-clip pages particularly important to you. This book was written to help support you in moments of doubt and indecision. After several readings, you may only need to scan the "Action" suggestions or flip to the motto at the end of each chapter in order to set yourself on the right course again. Try reading one chapter a day at the start of your working day. Or review it at the end of your day—let the experiences of the day be assimilated into your joy of working philosophy.

This is *your* book to use every day of the month, every month of the year, every year of your working life.

We hope that you'll have reason to rejoice every day upon awaking. That your life will be enriched with a sense of purpose. That your growing philosophy about work will carry you through difficult days as well as the ones filled with song.

The joy of working is you. As you're doing your work, bring to it your unique being—a most valuable person endowed with faith, determination, and goodwill. Your inner joy will radiate cheer and confidence to all whose lives you touch in your working day.

You're getting the idea now. You've got the joy of working.

Denis Waitley and Reni Witt are available for speaking engagements on the general subject of the joy of working. For information on scheduling such appearances as well as audio, video, film and multi-media presentations, educational seminars, motivational workshops, training programs, and merchandising opportunities, please call or write:

Larimi Communications
Department 11
246 West 38th Street
New York, NY 10018

(212) 819-9300